STUDIES IN BUDDHISM

STUDIES IN BUDDHISM

BY

F. MAX MULLER
MONIER WILLIAMS
REGINALD STEPHEN
ROBERT C. CHILDERS

GYAN

Published by

GYAN

Gyan Publishing House
5, Ansari Road
Daryaganj, New Delhi-110002
Phone: 011-47034999, 9811692060
E-mail: books@gyanbooks.com

Distribution Network
gyanbooks.com
India, USA, Canada, UK, Australia, France

ISBN : 978-81-212-4075-8 (PB)
First Published, 1895

2nd Impression 2020

Printed at: Gyan Press, Delhi.

Studies in Buddhism
Author: F. Max Muller

PUBLISHERS' NOTE

The contents of this volume represent articles from the pens of F. Max Muller, Monier Williams, Reginald Stephen and Robert C. Childers. All of them appeared in books and periodicals which were published towards the later part of the nineteenth century.

The first five chapters are drawn from the writings of F. Max Muller and printed in his *Selected Essays,* Vol. II, 1881: *Buddha and Buddhism* is an extract from a review of J. Barthelemy Saint-Hilaire's *Le Bouddha et sa Religion,* Paris, 1860; *Buddhist Pilgrims* is a portion from a review of *Voyages des Pelerins Buddhistes,* a French translation of the *Life and Travel of Hiouen-Thsang* by Stanisles-Julien, Vols. I and II, Paris, 1853—1857; *The Meaning of Nirvana* first appeared as a letter to *The Times,* London, 1868. *Buddhist Nihilism* was a lecture delivered before a meeting of the Association of German Philologists in 1869; *Christianity and Buddhism* was published in the *Nineteenth Century* in 1891.

Monier Williams contributed his article *Buddhism and Jainism* to *The Contemporary Review,* 1882. *Buddhism in Ceylon* by Reginald Stephen appeared in *The Nineteenth Century,* 1888. The concluding article from the pen of Robert C. Childers is reproduced from *The Contemporary Review,* 1890.

CONTENTS

CHAPTER I.

BUDDHA AND BUDDHISM

Buddha, or more correctly, the Buddha—for Buddha is an appellative meaning Enlightened—was born at Kapilavastu, the capital of a kingdom of the same name, situated at the foot of the mountains of Nepal, north of the present Oude. His father, the king of Kapilavastu, was of the family of the Sakyas, and belonged to the clan of the Gautamas. His mother was Mayadevi, daughter of king Suprabuddha, and need we say that she was as beautiful as he was powerful and just ? Buddha was therefore by birth of the Kshatriya, or warrior caste, and he took the name of Sakya from his family, and that of Gautama from his clan, claiming a kind of spiritual relationship with the honoured race of Gautama. The name of Buddha, or the Buddha, dates from a later period of his life, and so probably does the name Siddhartha (he whose objects have been accomplished), though we are told that it was given him in his childhood. His mother died seven days after his birth, and the father confided the child to the care of his deceased wife's sister, who, however, had been his wife even before the mother's death. The child grew up a most beautiful and most accomplished boy, who soon knew more than his masters could teach him. He refused to take part in the games of his playmates, and never felt so happy as when he could sit alone, lost in meditation in the deep shadows of the forest. It was there that his father found him when he had thought him lost, and in order to prevent the young prince from becoming a dreamer, the king determined to marry him at once. When the subject was mentioned by the aged ministers to the future heir to the throne, he demanded seven days for reflection, and convinced at last that not even marriage could disturb the calm of his mind, he allowed the ministers to look out for a princess. The princess selected was the beautiful Gopa, the daughter of Dandapani. Though her father objected at first to her marrying a young prince who was represented to him as deficient in manliness and intellect, he gladly gave his consent when he saw the royal suitor distancing all his rivals both in feats of arms and power of mind. Their marriage proved one of the happiest, but the prince remained, as he had been before, absorbed in meditation on the problems of life and death. 'Nothing is stable on earth,' he used to say, 'nothing is real. Life is like the spark produced by the friction of wood. It is lighted and is extinguished—we know not whence it came or whither it goes. It is like the sound of a lyre, and the wise man asks in vain from whence it came and whither it goes. There must be some supreme intelligence where we could find rest. If I attained it, I could bring light to man; if I were free myself, I could deliver the world.' The king, who perceived the melancholy mood of the young prince, tried everything to divert him from his speculations : but all was in vain. Three of the most ordinary events that could happen to any man proved of the utmost importance in the career of Buddha. We quote the description of these occurrences from Barthelemy Saint-Hilaire :

'One day when the prince with a large retinue was driving through the eastern gate of the city on the way to one of his parks, he met on the road an old man, broken and decrepit. One could see the veins and muscles over the whole of his body; his teeth chattered, he was covered with wrinkles, bald, and hardly able to utter hollow and unmelodious sounds. He was bent on his stick, and all his limbs and joints trembled. "Who is that man ?" said the prince to his coachman. "He is small and weak, his flesh and his blood are dried up, his muscles stick to his skin, his head is white, his teeth chatter, his body is wasted away; leaning on his stick he is hardly able to walk, stumbling at every step. Is there something peculiar in his family, or is this the common lot of all created beings ? "

'"Sir," replied the coachman, "that man is sinking under old age, his senses have become obtuse, suffering has destroyed his strength, and he is despised by his relations. He is without support and useless, and people have abandoned him like a dead tree in a forest. But this is not peculiar to his family. In every creature youth is defeated by old age. Your father, your mother, all your relations, all your friends, will come to the same state; this is the appointed end of all creatures."

'"Alas !" replied the prince, "are creatures so ignorant, so weak and foolish, as to be proud of the youth by which they are intoxicated, not seeing the old age which awaits them! As for me, I go away. Coachman, turn my chariot quickly. What have I, the future prey of old age—what have I to do with pleasure?" And the young prince returned to the city without going to his park.

'Another time the prince was driving through the southern gate to his pleasure garden, when he perceived on the road a man suffering from illness, parched with fever, his body wasted, covered with mud, without a friend, without a home, hardly able to breathe, and frightened at the sight of himself and the approach of death. Having questioned his coachman, and received from him the answer which he expected, the young prince said, "Alas! health is but the sport of a dream, and the fear of suffering must take this frightful form. Where is the wise man who, after having seen what he is, could any longer think of joy and pleasure?" The prince turned his chariot and returned to the city.

'A third time he was driving to his pleasure garden through the western gate, when he saw a dead body on the road, lying on a bier, and covered with a cloth. The friends stood about crying, sobbing, tearing their hair, covering their heads with dust, striking their breasts and uttering wild cries. The prince, again, calling his coachman to witness this painful scene, exclaimed, "Oh! woe to youth, which must be destroyed by old age! Woe to health, which must be destroyed by so many diseases! Woe to this life, where a man remains so short a time! If there were no old age, no disease, no death; if these could be made captive for ever!" Then, betraying for the first time his intentions, the young prince said, "Let us turn back: I must think how to accomplish deliverance."

'A last meeting put an end to his hesitation. He was driving through the northern gate on the way to his pleasure gardens, when he saw a mendicant who appeared outwardly calm, subdued, looking downwards, wearing with an air of dignity his religious vestment, and carrying an alms-bowl.

'"Who is this man?" asked the prince.

'"Sir," replied the coachman, "this man is one of those who are called bhikshus, or mendicants. He has renounced all pleasures, all desires, and leads a life of austerity. He tries to conquer himself. He has become a devotee. Without passion, without envy, he walks about asking for alms."

'"This is good and well said," replied the prince. "The life of a devotee has always been praised by the wise. It will be my refuge, and the refuge of other creatures; it will lead us to a real life, to happiness and immortality."

'With these words the young prince turned his chariot and returned to the city.'

After having declared to his father and his wife his intention of retiring from the world, Buddha, in spite of their remonstrances, left his palace one night when all the guards that were to have watched him were asleep. After travelling the whole night, he gave his horse and his ornaments to his groom, and sent him back to Kapilavastu. 'A monument,' remarks the author of the Lalita-Vistara, 'is still to be seen on the spot where the coachman turned back.' Hiouen-Thsang saw the same monument at the edge of a large forest, on his road to Kusinagara, a city now in ruins, and situated about fifty miles E.S.E. from Gorakpur.[1]

Buddha first went to Vaisali, and became the pupil of a famous Brahman, who had gathered round him 300 disciples. Having learnt all that the Brahman could teach him, Buddha went away disappointed. He had not found the road to salvation. He then tried another Brahman at Rajagriha, the capital of Magadha or Behar, who had 700 disciples, and there too he looked in vain for the means of deliverance. He left him, followed by five of his fellow-students, and for six years retired into solitude, near a village named Uruvilva, subjecting himself to the most severe penances, previous to his appearing in the world as a teacher. At the end of this period, however, he arrived at the conviction that asceticism, far from giving peace of mind and preparing the way to salvation, was a snare and a stumbling-block in the way of truth. He gave up his exercises, and was at once deserted as an apostate by his five disciples. Left to himself, he now began to elaborate his own system.

[1] The geography of India at the time of Buddha, and later at the time of Fahian and Hiouen-Thsang, has been admirably treated by L. Vivien de Saint-Martin, in his 'Mémoire Analytique sur la Carte de l'Asie Centrale et de l'Inde,' in the third volume of Stanislas Julien's *Pèlerins Bouddhistes*.

He had learnt that neither the doctrines nor the austerities of the Brahmans were of any avail for accomplishing the deliverance of man, and freeing him from the fear of old age, disease, and death. After long meditations, and ecstatic visions, he at last imagined that he had arrived at that true knowledge which discloses the cause, and thereby destroys the fear, of all the changes inherent in life. It was from the moment when he arrived at this knowledge, that he claimed the name of Buddha, the Enlightened. At that moment we may truly say that the fate of millions of millions of human beings trembled in the balance. Buddha hesitated for a time whether he should keep his knowledge to himself—remain, in fact, a Pratyeka-buddha—or communicate it to the world. Compassion for the sufferings of man prevailed, and the young prince became the founder of a religion which, after more than 2,000 years, is still professed by a larger number of human beings than any other religion.

The further history of the new teacher is very simple. He proceeded to Benares, which at all times was the principal seat of learning in India, and the first converts he made were the five fellow-students who had left him when he threw off the yoke of the Brahmanical observances. Many others followed; but as the Lalita-Vistara breaks off at Buddha's arrival at Benares, we have no further consecutive account of the rapid progress of his doctrine. From what we can gather from scattered notices in the Buddhist canon, he was invited by the king of Magadha, Bimbisara, to his capital, Rajagriha. Many of his lectures are represented as having been delivered at the monastery of Kalantaka, with which the king or some rich merchant had presented him; others on the Vulture Peak, one of the five hills that surrounded the ancient capital.

Three of his most famous disciples, Sariputra, Katyayana, and Maudgalyayana, joined him during his stay in Magadha, where he enjoyed for many years the friendship of the king. That king was afterwards assassinated by his son, Ajatasatru, and then we hear of Buddha as settled for a time at Sravasti, north of the Ganges, where Anathapindada, a rich merchant, had offered him and his disciples a magnificent building for their residence. Most of Buddha's lectures or sermons were delivered at Sravasti, the capital of Kosala; and the king of Kosala himself, Prasenajit, became a convert to his doctrine. After an absence of twelve years we are told that Buddha visited his father at Kapilavastu, on which occasion he is said to have performed several miracles, and converted all the Sakyas to his faith. His own wife became one of his followers, and, with his aunt, offers the first instance of female Buddhist devotees in India. We have fuller particulars again of the last days of Buddha's life. He had attained the good age of three score and ten, and had been on a visit to Rajagriha, where the king, Ajatasatru, the former enemy of Buddha, and the assassin of his own father, had joined the congregation, after making a public confession of his crimes. On his return he was followed by a large number of disciples, and when on the point of crossing the Ganges, he stood on a square stone, and turning his eyes back towards Rajagriha, he said, full of emotion, 'This is the last time that I see that city.' He likewise visited Vaisali, and after taking leave of it, he had nearly reached the city of Kusinagara, when his vital strength began to fail. He halted in a forest, and while sitting under a sal tree, he gave up the ghost, or, as a Buddhist would say, attained Nirvana. This is the simple story of Buddha's life.

Making every possible allowance for the accumulation of fiction[2] which is sure to gather round the life of the founder of every great religion, we may be satisfied that Buddhism, which changed the aspect not only of India, but of nearly the whole of Asia, had a real founder; that he was not a Brahman by birth, but belonged to the second or royal caste; that being of a meditative turn of mind, and deeply impressed with the frailty of all created things, he became a recluse, and sought for light and comfort in the different systems of Brahman philosophy and theology. Dissatisfied with the artificial systems of their priests and philosophers; convinced of the uselessness, nay of the pernicious influence, of their ceremonial practices and bodily penances; shocked, too, by their worldliness and pharisaical conceit, which made the priesthood the exclusive property of one caste and rendered every pious act impossible without their intervention, Buddha must have produced at once

[2] This subject has since been fully and carefully treated by Senart, in his *Essai sur la Légende du Buddha*, Paris, 1875.

a powerful impression on the people at large, when, breaking through all the established rules of caste, he assumed the privileges of a Brahman, and, throwing away the splendour of his royal position, travelled about as a beggar, not shrinking from the defiling contact of sinners and publicans. Though when we now speak of Buddhism we think chiefly of its doctrines, the reform of Buddha had originally much more of a social than of a religious character. Buddha swept away the web with which the Brahmans had encircled the whole of India. Beginning as the reformer of an old, he became the founder of a new religion. We can hardly understand how any nation could have lived under a system like that of the Brahmanic hierarchy, which coiled itself round every public and private act, and would have rendered life intolerable to any who had forfeited the favour of their priests. That system was attacked by Buddha. Buddha might have taught whatever philosophy he pleased, and we should hardly have heard his name. The people would not have minded him, and his system would only have been a drop in the ocean of philosophical speculation by which India was deluged at all times. But when a young prince assembled round him people of all castes, of all ranks; when he defeated the Brahmans in public disputations; when he declared the sacrifices by which they made their living not only useless but sinful; when instead of severe penance or excommunications inflicted by the Brahmans sometimes for the most trifling offences, he only required public confession of sin and a promise to sin no more; when the charitable gifts hitherto monopolised by the Brahmans began to flow into new channels, supporting hundreds and thousands of Buddhist mendicants, more had been achieved than probably Buddha himself had ever dreamt of; and he whose meditations had been how to deliver the soul of man from misery and the fear of death, had delivered the people of India from a degrading thraldom and from priestly tyranny.

The most important element of the Buddhist reform has always been its social and moral code, not its metaphysical theories. That moral code, taken by itself, is one of the most perfect which the world has ever known. On this point all testimonies from hostile and from friendly quarters agree.

Buddhism became the state religion of India at the time of Asoka; and Asoka, the Buddhist Constantine, was the grandson of Chandragupta, and Chandragupta was the contemporary of Seleucus Nicator. The system of the Brahmans had run its course. Their ascendency, at first purely intellectual and religious, had gradually assumed a political character. By means of the system of caste this influence pervaded the whole social fabric, not as a vivifying leaven, but as a deadly poison. Their increasing power and self-confidence are clearly exhibited in the successive periods of their ancient literature. It begins with the simple hymns of the Veda. These are followed by the tracts known by the name of Brahmanas, in which a complete system of theology is elaborated and claims advanced in favour of the Brahmans such as were seldom conceded to any hierarchy. The third period in the history of their ancient literature is marked by their Sutras or Aphorisms, short and dry formularies, showing the Brahmans in secure possession of all their claims. Such privileges as they then enjoyed are never enjoyed for any length of time. It was impossible for anybody to move or to assert his freedom of thought and action without finding himself impeded on all sides by the web of the Brahmanic law; nor was there anything in their religion to satisfy the natural yearnings of the human heart after spiritual comfort. What was felt by Buddha had been felt more or less intensely by thousands; and this was the secret of his success. That success, however, was probably accelerated by political events. Chandragupta had conquered the throne of Magadha, and acquired his supremacy in India in defiance of the Brahmanic law. He was of low origin, a mere adventurer, and by his accession to the throne an important mesh had been broken in the intricate system of caste. Neither he nor his successors could count on the hearty support of the Brahmans, and it is but natural that his grandson, Asoka, should have been driven to seek support from the new sect founded by Buddha. Buddha, by giving up his royal station, had broken the law of caste as much as Chandragupta by usurping it. His school, though it had probably escaped open persecution until it rose to political importance, could never have been on friendly terms with the Brahmans of the old school. The *parvenu* on the throne saw his natural allies in the followers of Buddha, and the mendicants, who by their unostentatious behaviour had won golden opinions among the lower and middle classes, were suddenly raised to an importance little dreamt of by their founder. Those who see in Buddhism not a social but chiefly a religious and philosophical reform, have been deceived by the later Buddhist literature, and particularly by the controversies between Buddhists and Brahmans, which in later times led to the total expulsion of the former from India, and to the political re-establishment of Brahmanism. These, no doubt, turn chiefly on philosophical problems, and are of the most abstruse and intricate character. But such was not the teaching of Buddha. If we may judge from 'the four verities,' which Buddha inculcated from the first day that he entered on his career as a teacher, his philosophy of life was very simple. He proclaims that there was nothing but sorrow in life; that sorrow is produced by our affections, that our affections must be destroyed in order to destroy the root of sorrow, and that he could teach mankind how to eradicate all the affections, all passions, all desires. Such doctrines were intelligible; and considering that Buddha received people of all castes, who after renouncing the world and assuming their yellow robes were sure of finding a livelihood from the charitable gifts of the people, it is not surprising that the number of his followers should have grown so rapidly. If Buddha really taught the metaphysical doctrines which are ascribed to him by subsequent writers—and this is a point which it is impossible as yet to settle—not one in a thousand among his followers would have been capable of appreciating those speculations. They must have been reserved for a few of his disciples, and they would never have formed the nucleus for a popular religion.

There are no doubt certain notions which Buddha shares in common, not only with Kapila, but with every Hindu philosopher. The idea of transmigration, the belief in the continuing effects of our good and bad actions, extending from our former to our present and from our present to our future lives, the sense that life is a dream or a burden, the admission of the uselessness of religious observances after the attainment of the highest knowledge—all these belong, so to say, to the national philosophy of India. We meet with these ideas everywhere, in the poetry, the philosophy, the religion of the Hindus. They cannot be claimed as the exclusive property of any system in particular. But if we look for more special coincidences between Buddha's doctrines and those of Kapila or other Indian philosophers, we look in vain. At first it might seem as if the very first aphorism of Kapila—namely, 'the complete cessation of pain, which is of three kinds, is the highest aim of man'—was merely a philosophical paraphrase of the events which, as we saw, determined Buddha to renounce the world in search of the true road to salvation. But though the starting-point of Kapila and Buddha is the same, a keen sense of human misery and a yearning after a better state, their roads from the very first diverge so completely and their goals are so far apart, that it is difficult to understand how, almost by common consent, Buddha is supposed either to have followed in the footsteps of Kapila, or to have changed Kapila's philosophy into a religion. Some scholars imagine that there was a more simple and primitive philosophy which was taught by Kapila, and that the Sutras which are now ascribed to him are of later date. It is as easy to make as it is impossible either to prove or to disprove such an assertion. At present we know Kapila's philosophy from his Sutras only,[3] and these Sutras seem to us posterior, not anterior, to Buddha. Though the name of Buddha is not mentioned in the Sutras, his doctrines, I believe, are clearly alluded to and controverted in several parts of them.

It has been said that Buddha and Kapila were both atheists, and that Buddha borrowed his atheism from Kapila. But atheism is an indefinite term, and may mean very different things. In one sense every Indian philosopher was an atheist, for they all perceived that the gods of the populace could not claim the attributes that belong to a Supreme Being. But all the important philosophical systems of the Brahmans admit, in some form or other, the existence of an Absolute and Supreme Being, the source of all that exists, or seems to exist. Kapila, when accused of atheism, is not accused of denying the existence of an Absolute Being. He is accused of denying the existence of an Isvara, which in general means the Lord, but which, in the passage where it occurs, refers to the Isvara of the Yogins, or

[3] Of Kapila's Sutras, together with the commentary of Vijnana Bhikshu, a new edition was published in 1856, by Fitz-Edward Hall, in the *Bibliotheca Indica*. An excellent translation of the Aphorisms, with illustrative extracts from the commentaries, was printed for the use of the Benares College, by Ballantyne.

mystic philosophers. These Yogins maintained that in an ecstatic state man possesses the power of seeing God face to face, and they wished to have this ecstatic intuition included under the head of sensuous perceptions. To this Kapila demurred. You have not proved the existence of your Lord, he says, and therefore I see no reason why I should alter my definition of sensuous perception in order to accommodate your ecstatic visions. The commentator narrates that this strong language was used by Kapila in order to silence the wild talk of the Mystics, and that, though he taunted his adversaries with having failed to prove the existence of their Lord, he himself was far from denying the existence of a Supreme Being. Kapila, however, went further. He endeavoured to show that all the attributes which the Mystics ascribed to their Lord are inappropriate. He used arguments very similar to those which have lately been used with such ability by a distinguished Bampton Lecturer. The Supreme Lord of the Mystics, Kapila argued, is either absolute and unconditioned (mukta), or he is bound and conditioned (baddha). If he is absolute and unconditioned, he cannot enter into the condition of a Creator; he would have no desires which could instigate him to create. If, on the contrary, he is represented as active, and entering on the work of creation, he would no longer be the absolute and unchangeable Being which we are asked to believe in. Kapila, like the preacher of our own days, was accused of paving the road to atheism, but his philosophy was nevertheless admitted as orthodox, because, in addition to sensuous perception and inductive reasoning, Kapila professed emphatically his belief in revelation—**i.e.** in the Veda—and allowed to it a place among the recognised instruments of knowledge. Buddha refused to allow to the Vedas any independent authority whatever, and this constituted the fundamental difference between the two philosophers.

Whether Kapila's philosophy was really in accordance with the spirit of the Veda, is quite a different question. No philosophy, at least nothing like a definite system, is to be found in the sacred hymns of the Brahmans; and though the Vedanta philosophy does less violence than the Sankhya to what it quotes from the Veda, the authors of the Veda woulo have been as much surprised at the consequences deduceo from their words by the Vedantin as by the strange meaning attributed to them by Kapila. The Vedanta philosopher would deny the existence of a Creator in the usual sense of the word quite as much as the follower of the Sankhya philosophy of Kapila. He explained the universe as an emanation from Brahman, which is all in all, not as the creation of a God. Kapila admitted two principles, an absolute Spirit and Nature, and he looked upon the universe as produced by a reflection of Nature thrown on the mirror of the absolute Spirit. Both systems seem to regard creation, or the created world, as an unfortunate accident. But they maintain that its effects can be neutralised, and that emancipation from the bonds of earthly existence is possible by means of philosophy. The Vedanta philosopher imagined that he was free when he had arrived at the knowledge that nothing exists but Brahman; that all phenomena are merely the result of ignorance; that after the destruction of that ignorance, and of its effects, all is merged again in Brahman, the true source of being, thought, and happiness. Kapila taught that the spirit became free from all mundane fetters as soon as it perceived that all phenomena were only passing reflections produced by nature upon the spirit, and as soon as it was able to shut its eyes to those illusory visions. Both systems, therefore—and the same applies to all the other philosophical systems of the Brahmans—admitted an absolute or self-existing Being, as the cause of all that exists or seems to exist. And here lies the specific difference between Kapila and Buddha. Buddha, like Kapila, maintained that this world had no absolute reality, that it was a snare and an illusion. The words, 'All is perishable, all is miserable, all is void,' must frequently have passed his lips. But we cannot call things unreal unless we have a conception of something that is real. Where, then, did Buddha find a reality in comparison with which this world might be called unreal ? What remedy did he propose as an emancipation from the sufferings of this life ? Difficult as it seems to us to conceive it, Buddha admits of no real cause of this unreal world. He denies the existence not only of a Creator, but of any Absolute Being. According to the metaphysical tenets, if not of Buddha himself, at least of his sect, there is no reality anywhere, neither in the past nor in the future. True wisdom consists in perceiving the nothingness of all things, and in a desire to become nothing, to be blown out, to enter into the state of Nirvana. Emancipation is obtained by total extinction, not by absorption in Brahman, or by a recovery of the soul's true estate. If to be is misery, not to be must be felicity; and this felicity is the highest reward which Buddha promised to his disciples. In reading the Aphorisms of Kapila, it is difficult not to see in his remarks on those who maintain that all is void, covered attacks on Buddha and his followers. In one place (I. 43) Kapila argues that if people believed in the reality of thought only, and denied the reality of external objects, they would soon be driven to admit that nothing at all exists, because we perceive our thoughts in the same manner as we perceive external objects.' This naturally leads him to an examination of that extreme doctrine according to which all that we perceive is void, and all is supposed to perish, because it is the nature of things that they should perish. Kapila remarks in reference to this view (I. 45), that it is a mere assertion of persons who are 'not enlightened'—in Sanskrit a-buddha, a sarcastic expression in which it is difficult not to see an allusion to Buddha, or to those who claimed for him the title of the Enlightened.[4] Kapila then proceeds to give the best answer that could be given to those who taught that complete annihilation must be the highest aim of man, as the only means of a complete cessation of suffering. 'It is not so,' he says, 'for if people wish to be free from suffering, it is they themselves who wish to be free, just as in this life it is they themselves who wish to enjoy happiness. There must be a permanent soul in order to satisfy the yearnings of the human heart, and if you deny that soul, you have no right to speak of the highest aim of man.'

Whether the belief in this kind of Nirvana—*i.e.* in a total extinction of being, personality, and consciousness—was at any time shared by the large masses of the people, is difficult either to assert or deny. We know nothing in ancient times of the religious convictions of the millions. We only know what a few leading spirits believed, or professed to believe. That certain people in modern and ancient times have spoken and written of total extinction as the highest aim of man cannot be denied. Job cursed the day on which he was born, and Solomon praised the 'dead which are already dead, more than the living which are yet

[4] For a similar play on the word Buddha, see Mahabhar., xv. 567.

alive.' 'Yea, better is he than both they,' he said, 'which hath not yet been, who hath not seen the evil work that is done under the sun.' Voltaire said in his own flippant way, 'On aime la vie, mais le neant ne laisse pas d'avoir du bon;' and a modern German philosopher, who has found much favour with those who profess to despise Kant, Schelling, and Hegel, writes, 'Considered in its objective value, it is more than doubtful that life is preferable to the Nothing. I should say even, that if experience and reflection could lift up their voices they would recommend to us the Nothing. We are what ought not to be, and we shall therefore cease to be.' Under peculiar circumstances, in the agonies of despair, or under the gathering clouds of madness, such language is intelligible : but to believe, as we are asked to believe, that one half of mankind had yearned for total annihilation would be tantamount to a belief that there is a difference in kind between man and man. Buddhist philosophers, no doubt, held this doctrine, and it cannot be denied that it found a place in the Buddhist canon. But even among the different schools of Buddhist philosophers, very different views are adopted as to the true meaning of Nirvana, and with the modern Buddhists of Burmah, for instance, Nigban, as they call it, is defined simply as freedom from old age, disease, and death. We do not find fault with Barthelemy Saint-Hilaire for having so emphatically pressed the charge of nihilism against Buddha himself. In one portion of the Buddhist canon the most extreme views of nihilism are put into his mouth. All we can say is that that canon is later than Buddha, and that in the canonical books of the Northern Buddhists, such as the 'Lotus of the Good Law,'[5] the founder of Buddhism, after having entered into Nirvana, is still spoken of as living, nay, as showing himself

[5]This statement has been fiercely attacked by D'Alwis, in his *Buddhist Nirvana*, p. 50. '"But," says Max Müller, "in the legends Buddha appears to his disciples even after his death." We confess we are utterly ignorant of the legend here referred to; but we are not a little surprised that a writer, who insists upon the Buddhist Canon alone as being our true guide in all matters, should refer to, or derive aid from, legendary tales in favour of this new doctrine of nihilism.' My answer is that in one of the canonical books of the Northern Buddhists, the Saddharma-pundarika, we read : 'When I (Bhagavat) shall have entered into complete Nirvana, I shall send numerous miracles;' and again, 'I shall then show my luminous form,' etc. See *Lotus de la bonne Loi*, p. 144.

to those who believe in him. Buddha, who denied the existence, or at least the divine nature, of the gods worshipped by the Brahmans, was raised himself to the rank of a deity by some of his followers[6] (the Aisvarikas), and we need not wonder, therefore, if his Nirvana too was gradually changed into an Elysian field.

And finally, if we may argue from human nature, such as we find it at all times and in all countries, we confess that we cannot bring ourselves to believe that the reformer of India, the teacher of so perfect a code of morality, the young prince who gave up all he had in order to help those whom he saw afflicted in mind, body, or estate, should have cared much about speculations which he knew would either be misunderstood, or not understood at all, by those whom he wished to benefit; that he should have thrown away one of the most powerful weapons in the hands of every religious teacher, the belief in a future life, and should not have seen that, if this life was sooner or later to end in nothing, it was hardly worth the trouble which he took himself, or the sacrifices which he imposed on his disciples.

[6] How early this took place, we see from Clemens of Alexandria, *Strom.* i, p. 305, A.B. (ed. Colon. 1688); *Megasthenis Indica*, ed. Schwanbeck, p. 139, *eisi de ton Indon hoi tois Boutta (Bouta) peithomenoi paraggelmasin, hon di huperbolen semnotetos hos theon tetimekasi.*

CHAPTER II

BUDDHIST PILGRIMS

In order to understand what Hiouen-Thsang was, and to appreciate his life and his labours, we must first cast a glance at the history of a religion which, however unattractive and even mischievous it may appear to ourselves, inspired her votary with the true spirit of devotion and self-sacrifice. That religion has now existed for 2,400 years. To millions and millions of human beings it has been the only preparation for a higher life placed within their reach. And even at the present day it counts in Asia a more numerous array of believers than any other faith, not excluding Mohammedanism or Christianity. The religion of Buddha took its origin in India about the middle of the sixth century B.C., but it did not assume its political importance till about the time of Alexander's invasion. We know little, therefore, of its first origin and spreading, because the canonical works on which we must chiefly rely for information belong to a later period, and are strongly tinged with a legendary character. The very existence of such a being as Buddha, the son of Suddhodana, king of Kapilavastu, has been doubted. But what can never be doubted is this, that Buddhism, such as we find it in Russia[1] and Sweden[2] on the very threshold of European civilisation, in the north of Asia, in Mongolia, Tatary, China, Tibet,

[1] See W. Spottiswoode's *Tarantasse Journey*, p. 220, Visit to the Buddhist Temple.

[2] The only trace of the influence of Buddhism among the Kudic races, the Fins, Laps, etc., is found in the name of their priests and sorcerers, the Shamans. Shaman, whatever has been said to the contrary, is a corruption of Sramana, a name applied to Buddha, and to Buddhist priests in general. The ancient mythological religion of the Kudic races has nothing in common with Buddhism. See Castrèn's *Lectures on Finnish Mythology*, 1853. Finland was ceded by Sweden to Russia in 1809. See the Author's *Survey of Languages*, second edition, p. 116. Shamanism found its way from India to Siberia *via* Tibet, China, and Mongolia. Rules on the formation of magic figures, on the treatment of diseases by charms, on the worship of evil spirits, on the acquisition of supernatural powers, on charms, incantations, and other branches of Shaman witchcraft, are found in the Stan-gyour, or the second part of the Tibetan canon, and in some of the late Tantras of the Nepalese collection.

Nepal, Siam, Burmah, and Ceylon, had its origin in India.[1] Doctrines similar to those of Buddha existed in that country long before his time. We can trace them like meandering roots below the surface long before we reach the point where the roots strike up into a stem, and the stem branches off again into fruit-bearing branches. What was original and new in Buddha was his changing a philosophical system into a practical doctrine; his taking the wisdom of the few, and coining as much of it as he thought genuine for the benefit of the many; his breaking with the traditional formalities of the past, and proclaiming for the first time, in spite of castes and creeds, the equality of the rich and the poor, the foolish and the wise, the 'twice-born' and the outcast. Buddhism, as a religion and as a political event, was a reaction against Brahmanism, though it retained much of that more primitive form of faith and worship. Buddhism, in its historical growth, presupposes Brahmanism, and, however hostile the mutual relation of these two religions may have been at different periods of Indian history, it can be shown, without much difficulty, that the latter was but a natural consequence of the former.

The ancient religion of the Aryan inhabitants of India had started, like the religion of the Greeks, the Romans, the Germans, Slaves, and Celts, with a simple and intelligible mythological phraseology. In the Veda—for there is but one real Veda—the names of all the so-called gods or Devas betray their original physical character and meaning without disguise. The fire was praised and invoked by the name of Agni (ignis); the earth by the name of Prithvi (the broad); the sky by the name of Dyu (Jupiter), and afterwards of Indra; the firmament and the waters by the name of Varuna or *Ouranos*. The sun was invoked by many names, such as Surya, Savitri, Vishnu or Mitra; and the dawn rejoiced in such titles as Ushas, Urvasi, Ahana, and Surya. Nor was the moon forgotten. For though it is mentioned but rarely under its usual name of Chandra, it is alluded to under the more sacred appellation of Soma; and each of its four phases had received its own denomination. There is hardly any

[1] The area of Buddhism includes vast territories, from Ceylon and the Indian Archipelago in the south to the Baikal Lake in Central Asia, and from the Caucasus eastward to Japan (Schlagintweit, *Buddhism in Tibet*, p. 10).

part of nature, if it could impress the human mind in any way with the ideas of a higher power, of order, eternity, or beneficence—whether the winds, or the rivers, or the trees, or the mountains—without a name and representative in the early Hindu Pantheon. No doubt there existed in the human mind, from the very beginning, something, whether we call it a suspicion, an innate idea, an intuition, or a sense of the Divine. What distinguishes man from the rest of the animal creation is chiefly that ineradicable feeling of dependence and reliance upon some higher power, a consciousness of bondage from which the very name of 'religion' was derived. 'It is He that hath made us, and not we ourselves.' The presence of that power was felt everywhere, and nowhere more clearly and strongly than in the rising and setting of the sun, in the change of day and night, of spring and winter, of birth and death. But, although the Divine presence was felt everywhere, it was impossible in that early period of thought, and with a language incapable as yet of expressing anything but material objects, to conceive the idea of God in its purity and fullness, or to assign to it an adequate and worthy expression. Children cannot think the thoughts of men, and the poets of the Veda could not speak the language of Aristotle. It was by a slow process that the human mind elaborated the idea of one absolute and supreme Godhead; and by a still slower process that the human language matured a word to express that idea. A period of growth was inevitable, and those who, from a mere guess of their own, do not hesitate to speak authoritatively of a primeval revelation which imparted to the Pagan world the idea of the Godhead in all its purity, forget that, however pure and sublime and spiritual that revelation might have been, there was no language capable as yet of expressing the high and immaterial conceptions of that Heaven-sent message. The real history of religion, during the earliest mythological period, represents to us a slow process of fermentation in thought and language, with its various interruptions, its overflowings, its coolings, its deposits, and its gradual clearing from all extraneous and foreign admixture. This is not only the case among the Indo-European or Aryan races in India, in Greece, and in Germany. In Peru, and wherever the primitive formations of the intellectual world crop out, the process is exactly the same. 'The religion of the sun,' as it has been boldly said by the author of the 'Spanish Conquest in America,' 'was inevitable.' It was like a deep furrow which that heavenly luminary drew, in its silent procession from east to west, over the virgin mind of the gazing multitude; and in the impression left there by the first rising and setting of the sun there lay the dark seed of a faith in a more than human being, the first intimation of a life without beginning, of a world without end. Manifold seed fell afterwards into the soil once broken. Something divine was discovered in everything that moved and lived. Names were stammered forth in anxious haste, and no single name could fully express what lay hidden in the human mind and wanted expression—the idea of an absolute, and perfect, and supreme, and immortal Being. Thus a countless host of nominal gods was called into existence, and for a time seemed to satisfy the wants of a thoughtless multitude. But there were thoughtful men at all times, and their reason protested against the contradictions of a mythological phraseology, though it had been hallowed by sacred customs and traditions. That rebellious reason had been at work from the very first, always ready to break the yoke of names and formulas which no longer expressed what they were intended to express. The idea which had yearned for utterance was the idea of a Supreme and Absolute Power, and that yearning was not satisfied by such names as Kronos, Zeus, and Apollon. The very sound of such a word as 'God' used in the plural jarred on the ear, as if we were to speak of two universes, or of a single twin. There are many words, as Greek and Latin grammarians tell us, which if used in the plural, have a different meaning from what they have in the singular. The Latin *œdes* means a temple; if used in the plural it means a house. *Deus* and *theos* ought to be added to the same class of words. The idea of supreme perfection excluded limitation, and the idea of God excluded the possibility of many gods. This may seem language too abstract and metaphysical for the early times of which we are speaking. But the ancient poets of the Vedic hymns have expressed the same thought with perfect clearness and simplicity. In the Rig-Veda[4] we read :

'That which is one the sages speak of in many ways—they call it Agni, Yama, Matarisvan.'

[4] I, 164, 46.

Besides the plurality of gods, which was sure to lead to their destruction, there was a taint of mortality which they could not throw off. They all derived their being from the life of nature. The god who represented the sun was liable, in the mythological language of antiquity, to all the accidents which threatened the solar luminary. Though he might rise in immortal youth in the morning, he was conquered by the shadows of the night, and the powers of winter seemed to overthrow his heavenly throne. There is nothing in nature free from change, and the gods of nature fell under the thraldom of nature's laws. The sun must set, and the solar gods and heroes must die. There must be one God, there must be one unchanging Deity; this was the silent conviction of the human mind. There are many gods, liable to all the vicissitudes of life; this was everywhere the answer of mythological religion.

It is curious to observe in how various ways these two opposite principles were kept for a time from open conflict, and how long the heathen temples resisted the enemy which was slowly and imperceptibly undermining their very foundations. In Greece this mortal element, inherent in all gods, was eliminated to a great extent by the conception of heroes. Whatever was too human in the ancient legends told of Zeus and Apollon was transferred to so-called half-gods or heroes, who were represented as the sons or favourites of the gods, and who bore their fate under a slightly altered name. The twofold character of Herakles as a god and as a hero is acknowledged even by Herodotus, and some of his epithets would have been sufficient to indicate his solar and originally divine character. But, in order to make some of the legends told of the solar deity possible or conceivable, it was necessary to represent Herakles as a more human being, and to make him rise to the seat of the Immortals only after he had endured toils and sufferings incompatible with the dignity of an Olympian god. We find the same idea in Peru, only that there it led to different results. A thinking—or, as he was called, a free-thinking—Inca[5] remarked that this perpetual travelling of the sun was a sign of servitude,[6] and he threw doubts upon the divine

[5] Helps, *The Spanish Conquest,* vol. iii, p. 503: 'Que cosa tam inquieta nou le parescia ser Dios.'

[6] On the servitude of the gods, see the Essay on Comparative Mythology, *Oxford Essays,* 1856, p. 69.

nature of such an unquiet thing as that great luminary appeared to him to be. And this misgiving led to a tradition which, even should it be unfounded in history, had some truth in itself, that there was in Peru an earlier worship, that of an invisible Deity, the Creator of the world, Pachacamac. In Greece, also, there are signs of a similar craving after the 'Unknown God.' A supreme God was wanted, and Zeus, the stripling of Creta, was raised to that rank. He became God above all gods—*hapanton kurios* as Pindar calls him. Yet more was wanted than a mere Zeus; and thus a Supreme Fate or Spell was imagined before which all the gods, and even Zeus, had to bow. And even this Fate was not allowed to remain supreme, and there was something in the destinies of man which was called *hupermoron* or 'beyond Fate.' The most awful solution, however, of the problem belongs to Teutonic mythology. Here, also, some heroes were introduced; but their death was only the beginning of the final catastrophe. 'All gods must die.' Such is the last word of that religion which had grown up in the forests of Germany, and found a last refuge among the glaciers and volcanoes of Iceland. The death of Sigurd, the descendant of Odin, could not avert the death of Balder, the son of Odin; and the death of Balder was soon to be followed by the death of Odin himself, and of all the immortal gods.

All this was inevitable, and Prometheus, the man of forethought, could safely predict the fall of Zeus. The struggles by which reason and faith overthrow tradition and superstition vary in different countries and at different times; but the final victory is always on their side. In India the same antagonism manifested itself, but what there seemed a victory of reason threatened to become the destruction of all religious faith. At first there was hardly a struggle. On the primitive mythological stratum of thought two new formations arose—the Brahmanical philosophy and the Brahmanical ceremonial; the one opening the widest avenues of philosophical thought, the other fencing all religious feeling within the narrowest barriers. Both derived their authority from the same source. Both professed to carry out the meaning and purpose of the Veda. Thus we see on the one side, the growth of a numerous and powerful priesthood, and the establishment of a ceremonial which embraced every moment of a man's life from his birth to his death. There was no event which might have moved the heart to a spontaneous outpouring of praise or thanksgiving which was not regulated by priestly formulas. Every prayer was prescribed, every sacrifice determined. Every god had his share, and the claims of each deity on the adoration of the faithful were set down with such punctiliousness, the danger of offending their pride was represented in such vivid colours, that no one would venture to approach their presence without the assistance of a well-paid staff of masters of divine ceremonies. It was impossible to avoid sin without the help of the Brahmans. They alone knew the food that might properly be eaten, the air which might properly be breathed, the dress which might properly be worn. They alone could tell what god should be invoked, what sacrifice be offered; and the slightest mistake of pronunciation, the slightest neglect about clarified butter, or the length of the ladle in which it was to be offered, might bring destruction upon the head of the unassisted worshipper. No nation was ever so completely priestridden as the Hindus were under the sway of the Brahmanic law. Yet, on the other side, the same people were allowed to indulge in the most unrestrained freedom of thought, and in the schools of their philosophy the very names of their gods were never mentioned. Their existence was neither denied nor asserted; they were of no greater importance in the system of the world of thought than trees or mountains, men or animals; and to offer sacrifices to them with a hope of rewards, so far from being meritorious, was considered as an impediment in the attainment of that emancipation to which a clear perception of philosophical truth was to lead the patient student. There was one system which taught that there existed but one Being, without a second; that everything else which seemed to exist was but a dream and illusion, and that this illusion might be removed by a true knowledge of the one Being. There was another system which admitted two principles—one a subjective and self-existent mind, the other matter, endowed with qualities. Here the world, with its joys and sorrows, was explained as the result of the subjective Self, reflecting itself in the mirror of matter; and final emancipation was obtained by turning away the eyes from the play of nature, and being absorbed in the knowledge of the true and absolute Self.

A third system started with the admission of atoms, and explained every effect, including the elements and the mind, animals, men, and gods, from the concurrence of these atoms. In fact, as Cousin remarked many years ago, the history of the philosophy of India is 'un abrege de l'histoire de la philosophie.' The germs of all these systems are traced back to the Vedas, Brahmanas, and the Upanishads, and the man who believed in any of them was considered as orthodox as the devout worshipper of the gods—the one was saved by knowledge and faith, the other by works and faith.

Such was the state of the Hindu mind when Buddhism arose; or, rather, such was the state of the Hindu mind which gave rise to Buddhism. Buddha himself went through the school of the Brahmans. He performed their penances, he studied their philosophy, and he at last claimed the name of the Buddha, or the Enlightened, when he threw away the whole ceremonial, with its sacrifices, superstitions, penances, and castes, as worthless, and changed the complicated systems of philosophy into a short doctrine of salvation. This doctrine of salvation has been called pure Atheism and Nihilism, and it no doubt was liable to both charges in its metaphysical character, and in that form in which we chiefly know it. It was atheistic, not because it denied the existence of such gods as Indra and Brahma. Buddha did not even condescend to deny their existence. But it was called atheistic, like the Sankhya philosophy, which admitted but one subjective Self, and considered creation as an illusion of that Self, imagining itself for a while in the mirror of nature. As there was no reality in creation, there could be no real Creator. All that seemed to exist was the result of ignorance. To remove that ignorance was to remove the cause of all that seemed to exist. How a religion which taught the annihilation of all existence, of all thought, of all individuality and personality, as the highest object of all endeavours, could have laid hold of the minds of millions of human beings, and how at the same time, by enforcing the duties of morality, justice, kindness, and self-sacrifice, it could have exercised a decidedly beneficial influence, not only on the natives of India, but on the lowest barbarians of Central Asia, is a riddle which no one has as yet been able to solve.

We must distinguish, it seems, between Buddhism as a religion and Buddism as a philosophy. The former addressed itself to millions, the latter to a few isolated thinkers. It is from these isolated thinkers, however, and from their literary compositions, that we are apt to form our notions of what Buddhism was, while, as a matter of fact, not one in a thousand would have been capable of following these metaphysical speculations. To the people at large Buddhism was a moral and religious, not a philosophical reform. Yet even its morality has a metaphysical tinge. The morality which it teaches is not a morality of expediency and rewards. Virtue is not enjoined because it necessarily leads to happiness. No; virtue is to be practised, but happiness is to be shunned, and the only reward for virtue is that it subdues the passions, and thus prepares the human mind for that knowledge which is to end in complete annihilation. There are ten commandments which Buddha imposes on his disciples.[7] They are—

1. Not to kill.
2. Not to steal.
3. Not to commit adultery.
4. Not to lie.
5. Not to get intoxicated.
6. To abstain from unseasonable meals.
7. To abstain from public spectacles.
8. To abstain from expensive dresses.
9. Not to have a large bed.
10. Not to receive silver or gold.

The duties of those who embraced a religious life were more severe. They were not allowed to wear any dress except rags collected in cemeteries, and these rags they had to sew together with their own hands. A yellow cloak was to be thrown over these rags. Their food was to be extremely simple, and they were not to possess anything except what they could get by collecting alms from door to door in their wooden bowls. They had but one meal in the morning, and were not allowed to touch any food after midday. They were to live in forests, not in cities, and their only shelter was to be the shadow of a tree. There they were to sit, to

[7] See Burnouf, *Lotus de la bonne Loi*, p. 444. Barthelemy Saint-Hilaire, *Du Bouddhisme*, p. 132. Ch. F. Neumann, *Catechism of the Shamans*.

spread their carpet, but not to lie down, even during sleep. They were allowed to enter the nearest city or village in order to beg, but they had to return to their forest before night, and the only change which was allowed, or rather prescribed, was when they had to spend some nights in the cemeteries, there to meditate on the vanity of all things. And what was the object of all this asceticism ? Simply to guide each individual towards that path which would finally bring him to Nirvana, it may be, to utter extinction or annihilation. The very definition of virtue was that it helped man to cross over to the other shore, and that other shore was not death, but cessation of all being. Thus charity was considered a virtue; modesty, patience, courage, contemplation, and science, all were virtues, but they were practised only as a means of arriving at deliverance. Buddha himself exhibited the perfection of all these virtues. His charity knew no bounds. When he saw a tigress starved, and unable to feed her cubs, he is said to have made a charitable oblation of his body to be devoured by them. Hiouen-Thsang visited the place on the banks of the Indus where this miracle was supposed to have happened, and he remarks that the soil is still red there from the blood of Buddha, and that the trees and flowers have the same colour.[8] As to the modesty of Buddha, nothing could exceed it. One day, king Prasenajit, the protector of Buddha, called on him to perform miracles, in order to silence his adversaries, the Brahmans. Buddha consented. He performed the required miracles, but he exclaimed : 'Great king, I do not teach the law to my pupils, telling them, Go, ye saints, and before the eyes of the Brahmans and householders perform, by means of your supernatural powers, miracles greater than any man can perform. I tell them, when I teach them the law, Live, ye saints, hiding your good works and showing your sins.' And yet, all this self-sacrificing charity, all this self-sacrificing humility, by which the life of Buddha was distinguished throughout, and which he preached to the multitudes that came to listen to him, had, we are told, but one object, and that object was final annihilation. It is impossible almost to believe it, and yet when we turn away our eyes from the pleasing picture of that high morality which Buddha preached for

[8] Vol. i, p. 89, vol. ii, p. 167.

the first time to all classes of men, and look into the dark pages of his code of religious metaphysics, we can hardly find another explanation. Fortunately, the millions who embraced the doctrines of Buddha, and were saved by it from the depths of barbarism, brutality, and selfishness, were unable to fathom the meaning of his metaphysical doctrines. With them the Nirvana to which they aspired, became only a relative deliverance from the miseries of human life ; nay, it soon took the bright colours of a paradise to be regained by the pious worshipper of Buddha. But was this the meaning of Buddha himself ? In his 'Four Verities' he does not, indeed, define Nirvana, except by cessation of all pain; but when he traces the cause of pain, and teaches the means of destroying, not only pain itself, but the cause of pain, we shall see that his Nirvana assumes a very different meaning. His 'Four Verities' are very simple. The first asserts the existance of pain ; the second asserts that the cause of pain lies in sin ; the third asserts that pain may cease by Nirvana ; the fourth shows the way that leads to Nirvana. This way to Nirvana consists in eight things—right faith (orthodoxy), right judgment (logic), right language (veracity), right purpose (honesty), right practice (religious life), right obedience (lawful life), right remembrance, and right meditation. All these precepts might be understood as part of a simply moral code, closing with a kind of mystic meditation on the highest object of thought, and with a yearning after deliverance from all worldly ties. Similar systems have prevailed in many parts of the world, without a denial of the existence of an Absolute Being, or of a something towards which the human mind tends, in which it is absorbed or even annihilated. Awful as such a mysticism may appear, yet it leaves still something that exists, it acknowledges a feeling of dependence in man. It knows of a first cause, though it may have nothing to predicate of it except that it is *to kinoun akineton.* A return is possible from that desert. The first cause may be called to life again. It may take the names of Creator, Preserver, Ruler; and when the simplicity and helplessness of the child have re-entered the heart of man, the name of father will come back to the lips which had uttered in vain all the names of a philosophical despair. But from the Nirvana of the Buddhist metaphysician there is no return. He starts from the idea that the highest object is to escape pain. Life in his eyes is nothing but misery; birth the cause of all evil, from which even death cannot deliver him, because he believes in an eternal cycle of existence, or in transmigration. There is no deliverance from evil, except by breaking through the prison walls, not only of life, but of existence, and by extirpating the last cause of existence. What, then, is the cause of existence? The cause of existence, says the Buddhist metaphysician, is attachment—an inclination towards something; and this attachment arises from thirst or desire. Desire presupposes perception of the object desired; perception presupposes contact; contact, at least a sentient contact, presupposes the senses; and, as the senses can only perceive what has form and name, or what is distinct, distinction is the real cause of all the effects which end in existence, birth, and pain. Now, this distinction is itself the result of conceptions or ideas; but these ideas, so far from being, as in Greek philosophy, the true and everlasting forms of the Absolute, are here represented as mere illusions, the effects of ignorance (avidya). Ignorance, therefore, is really the primary cause of all that seems to exist. To know that ignorance, as the root of all evil, is the same as to destroy it, and with it all effects that flowed from it. In order to see how this doctrine affects the individual, let us watch the last moments of Buddha as described by his disciples. He enters into the first stage of meditation when he feels freedom from sin, acquires a knowledge of the nature of all things, and has no desire except that of Nirvana. But he still feels pleasure; he even uses his reasoning and discriminating powers. The use of these powers ceases in the second stage of meditation, when nothing remains but a desire after Nirvana, and a general feeling of satisfaction, arising from his intellectual perfection. That satisfaction, also, is extinguished in the third stage. Indifference succeeds; yet there is still self-consciousness, and a certain amount of physical pleasure. These last remnants are destroyed in the fourth stage; memory fades away, all pleasure and pain are gone, and the doors of Nirvana now open before him. After having passed these four stages once, Buddha went through them a second time, but he died before he attained again to the fourth stage. We must soar still higher, and though we may feel giddy and disgusted, we must sit out the tragedy till the curtain falls. After the four stages of meditation[9] are passed, the Buddha (and every being is to become a Buddha) enters into the infinity of space; then into the infinity of intelligence; and thence he passes into the region of nothing. But even here there is no rest. There is still something left—the idea of the nothing in which he rejoices. That also must be destroyed, and it is destroyed in the fourth and last region, where there is not even the idea of a nothing left, and where there is complete rest, undisturbed by nothing, or what is not nothing.[10] There are few persons who will take the trouble of reasoning out such hallucinations; least of all, persons who are accustomed to the sober language of Greek philosophy; and it is the more interesting to hear the opinion which one of the best Aristotelian scholars of the present day, after a patient examination of the authentic documents of Buddhism, has formed of its system of metaphysics. Barthelemy Saint-Hilaire, in a review on Buddhism, published in the 'Journal des Savants,' says :

'Buddhism has no God; it has not even the confused and vague notion of a Universal Spirit in which the human soul, according to the orthodox doctrine of Brahmanism, and the Sankhya philosophy, may be absorbed. Nor does it admit nature, in the proper sense of the word, and it ignores that profound division between spirit and matter which forms the system and the glory of Kapila. It confounds man with all that surrounds him, all the while preaching to him the laws of virtue. Buddhism, therefore, cannot unite the human soul, which it does not even mention, with a God, whom it ignores; nor with nature, which it does not know better. Nothing remained but to annihilate the soul; and in order to be quite sure that the soul may not re-appear under some new form in this world, which has been cursed as the abode of illusion and misery, Buddhism destroys its very elements, and never gets tired of glorying in this achievement. What more is wanted ? If this is not the absolute nothing, what is Nirvana ?'

[9] These 'four stages' are described in the same manner in the canonical books of Ceylon and Nepal, and may therefore safely be ascribed to that original form of Buddhism from which the southern and northern schools branched off at a later period. See Burnouf, *Lotus de la bonne Loi*, p. 800.

[10] See Burnouf, *ibid.*, p. 814.

Such religion, we should say, was made for a madhouse. But Buddhism was an advance, if compared with Brahmanism; it has stood its ground for centuries, and if truth could be decided by majorities, the show of hands, even at the present day, would be in favour of Buddha. The metaphysics of Buddhism, like the metaphysics of most religions, not excluding our own Gnosticism and Mysticism, were beyond the reach of all except a few hardened philosophers or ecstatic dreamers. Human nature could not be changed. Out of the very nothing it made a new paradise; and he who had left no place in the whole universe for a Divine Being, was deified himself by the multitudes who wanted a person whom they could worship, a king whose help they might invoke, a friend before whom they could pour out their most secret griefs. And there remained the code of a pure morality, proclaimed by Buddha. There remained the spirit of charity, kindness, and universal pity with which he had inspired his disciples.[11] There remained the simplicity of the ceremonial he had taught, the equality of all men which he had declared, the religious toleration which he had preached from the beginning. There remained much, therefore, to account for the rapid strides which his doctrine made from the mountain peaks of Ceylon to the Tundras of the Samoyedes, and we shall see in the simple story of the life of Hiouen-Thsang that Buddhism, with all its defects, has had its heroes, its martyrs, and its saints.

Hiouen-Thsang, born in China more than a thousand years after the death of Buddha, was a believer in Buddhism. He dedicated his whole life to the study of that religion; travelling from his native country to India, visiting every place mentioned in Buddhist history or tradition, acquiring the ancient language in which the canonical books of the Buddhists were written, studying commentaries, discussing points of difficulty, and defending the orthodox faith at

[11] See the 'Dhammapada,' a Pâli work on Buddhist ethics lately edited by V. Fausböll, a distinguished pupil of Professor Westergaard, at Copenhagen. Spence Hardy (*Eastern Monachism,* p. 169) writes: 'A collection might be made from the precepts of this work, that in the purity of its ethics could scarcely be equalled from any other heathen author.' Knighton, when speaking of the same work in his *History of Ceylon* (p. 77), remarks: 'In it we have exemplified a code of morality, and a list of precepts, which, for pureness, excellence, and wisdom, is only second to that of the Divine Lawgiver himself.'

public councils against disbelievers and schismatics. Buddhism had grown and changed since the death of its founder, but it had lost nothing of its vitality. At a very early period a proselytising spirit awoke among the disciples of the Indian reformer, an element entirely new in the history of ancient religions. No Jew, no Greek, no Roman, no Brahman ever thought of converting people to his own national form of worship. Religion was looked upon as private or national property. It was to be guarded against strangers. The most sacred names of the gods, the prayers by which their favour could be gained, were kept secret. No religion, however, was more exclusive than that of the Brahmans. A Brahman was born, nay, twice-born. He could not be made. Not even the lowest caste—that of the Sudras—would open its ranks to a stranger. Here lay the secret of Buddha's success. He addressed himself to castes and outcasts. He promised salvation to all; and he commanded his disciples to preach his doctrine in all places and to all men. A sense of duty, extending from the narrow limits of the house, the village, and the country to the widest circle of mankind, a feeling of sympathy and brotherhood towards all men—the idea, in fact, of humanity—was in India first pronounced by Buddha. In the third Buddhist Council, the acts of which have been preserved to us in the 'Mahavansa,'[12] we hear of missionaries being sent to the chief countries beyond India. This Council, we are told, took place 235 years after the death of Buddha, in the 17th year of the reign of the famous king Asoka, 242/308 B.C. whose edicts have been preserved to us on rock inscriptions in various parts of India. There are sentences in these inscriptions of Asoka which might be read with advantage by our own missionaries, though they are now more than 2,000 years old. Thus it is written on the rocks of Girnar, Dhauli, and Kapurdigiri[13]—

'Piyadasi, the king beloved of the gods, desires that the ascetics of all creeds might reside in all places. All these ascetics profess alike the command which people should

[12] *Mahavansa*, ed. G. Turnour, Ceylon, 1837, p. 71.

[13] Burgess, *Archæological Survey of Western India*, 1874-75, p. 110, tablet vii. Cunningham, *Corpus Inscriptionum Indicarum*, 1877, p. 121. Burnouf, *Lotus*, Appendice, p. 755.

exercise over themselves, and the purity of the soul. But people have different opinions, and different inclinations.'

And again[14] :

'Now, intrinsic worth can grow greater in many ways, but the foundation thereof, in all its compass, is discretion in speaking, so that no man may praise his own sect, or contemn another sect, or despise it on unsuitable occasions. On all occasions let respect be shown. Whatever of good, indeed, a man, from any motive, confers on any one of a different persuasion, tends to the advantage of his own sect and to the benefit of a different persuasion. By acting in an opposite manner, a man injures his own sect and offends a different sect..... Therefore, concord is best, so that all may know and willingly listen to each other's religion.'

Those who have no time to read the voluminous works of the late E. Burnouf on Buddhism, his 'Introduction a l'Histoire du Buddhisme,' and his translation of 'Le Lotus de la bonne Loi,' will find a very interesting and lucid account of these councils, and edicts and missions, and the history of Buddhism in general, in a work lately published by Charlotte Speir, 'Life in Ancient India.'[15] Buddhism spread in the south to Ceylon, in the north to Kashmir, the Himalayan countries, Tibet, and China. One Buddhist missionary is supposed to be mentioned in the Chinese annals as early as 217 B.C.;[16] and about 120 B.C. a Chinese general, after defeating the barbarous tribes north of the Desert of Gobi, brought back as a trophy a golden statue, the statue of Buddha.[17] It was not, however, till the year 65 A.D. that Buddhism was officially recognised by the Emperor Ming-ti[18] as a third state-religion in China. Ever since it has shared equal honours in the Celestial Empire, with the doctrines of Confucius and Lao-tse, and it is but lately that these three established religions have had to fear the encroachments of a new rival in the creed of the 'Chief of the Rebels.'

[14] Twelfth Tablet, Burgess, *l.c.*, p. 122; Cunningham, *l.c.*, p. 124. Translation by Kern.

[15] Also in a volume published by the Society for Promoting Christian Knowledge, *Buddhism*, by T. W. Rhys Davids, 1878.

[16] See *Foe Koue Ki*, p. 41, and xxxviii, preface.

[17] See *ibid.*, p. 41.

[18] *Lalita-Vistara*, ed. Foucaux, p. xvii, note.

After Buddhism had been introduced into China, the first care of its teachers was to translate the sacred works from Sanskrit, in which they were originally written, into Chinese. We read of the Emperor Ming-ti, of the dynasty of Han, sending Tsai-in and other high officials to India, in order to study there the doctrine of Buddha. They engaged the services of two learned Buddhists, Matanga and Chu-fa-lan, and some of the most important Buddhist works were translated by them into Chinese. 'The Life of Buddha,' the 'Lalita-Vistara,'[19] a Sanskrit work which, on account of its style and language, had been referred by Oriental scholars to a much more modern period of Indian literature, can now safely be ascribed to an ante-Christian era, if, as we are told by Chinese scholars, it was translated from Sanskrit into Chinese, as one of the canonical books of Buddhism, as early as the year 76 A.D.[20] The same work was translated also into Tibetan; and an edition of it, published in Paris by E. Foucaux, reflects high credit on that distinguished scholar, and on the Government which supports these studies in the most liberal and enlightened spirit. The intellectual intercourse between the Indian Peninsula and the northern continent of Asia remained uninterrupted for many centuries. Missions were sent from China to India, to report on the political and geographical state of the country, but the chief object of interest which attracted public embassies and private pilgrims across the Himalayan mountains was the religion of Buddha. About three hundred years after the public recognition of Buddhism by the Emperor Ming-ti, the great stream of Buddhist pilgrims began to flow from China to India. The first account which we possess of these pilgrimages refers to the travels of Fa-Hian, who visited India towards the end of the fourth century..... After Fa-Hian, we have the travels of Hoei-seng and Sung-yun[21] who were sent to India, in 518, by command of the Empress, with a view of collecting sacred books and relics..... After Hiouen-Thsang, the chief works of Chinese pilgrims are the 'Itineraries' of the fifty-six monks, published in 730, and the travels of Khi-nie, who visited India in 964, at the head

[19] This Sanskrit text has been published in the *Bibliotheca Indica*.

[20] This no longer holds good. Some Life of Buddha may have been translated at that early time, but there is no proof that it was the Lalita-Vistara, as we now possess it in Sanskrit.

[21] S. Beal has published an English translation of Fa-Hian and Sung-yun, 1869.

of three hundred pilgrims. India was for a time the Holy Land of China. There lay the scene of the life and death of the great teacher; there were the monuments commemorating the chief events of his life; there the shrines where his relics might be worshipped; there the monasteries where tradition had preserved his sayings and his doings; there the books where his doctrine might be studied in its original purity; there the schools where the tenets of different sects which had sprung up in the course of time might best be acquired.

Some of the pilgrims and envoys have left us accounts of their travels, and, in the absence of anything like an historical literature in India itself, these Chinese works are of the utmost importance for gaining an insight into the social, political, and religious history of that country from the beginning of our era to the time of the Mohammedan conquest.

We shall devote the rest of our space to a short account of the life and travels of Hiouen-Thsang. Hiouen-Thsang was born in a provincial town of China, at a time when the empire was in a chronic state of revolution. His father had left the public service, and had given most of his time to the education of his four children. Two of them distinguished themselves at a very early age—one of them was Hiouen-Thsang, the future traveller and theologian. The boy was sent to school at a Buddhist monastery, and, after receiving there the necessary instruction, partly from his elder brother, he was himself admitted as a monk at the early age of thirteen. During the next seven years, the young monk travelled about with his brother from place to place, in order to follow the lectures of some of the most distinguished professors. The horrors of war frequently broke in upon his quiet studies, and forced him to seek refuge in the more distant provinces of the empire. At the age of twenty he took priest's orders, and had then already become famous by his vast knowledge. He had studied the chief canonical books of the Buddhist faith, the records of Buddha's life and teaching, the system of ethics and metaphysics; and he was versed in the works of Confucius and Lao-tse. But still his own mind was agitated by doubts. Six years he continued his studies in the chief places of learning in China, and where he came to learn he was frequently asked to teach. At last, when he saw that none, even the most eminent theologians, were able to give him the information he wanted, he formed his resolve of travelling to India. The works of earlier pilgrims, such as Fa-Hian and others, were known to him. He knew that in India he should find the originals of the works which in their Chinese translation left so many things doubtful in his mind; and though he knew from the same sources the dangers of his journey, yet 'the glory,' as he says, 'of recovering the Law, which was to be a guide to all men and the means of their salvation, seemed to him worthy of imitation.' In common with several other priests, he addressed a memorial to the Emperor to ask leave for their journey. Leave was refused, and the courage of his companions failed. Not that of Hiouen-Thsang. His own mother had told him that, soon before she gave birth to him, she had seen her child travelling to the Far West in search of the Law. He was himself haunted by similar visions, and having long surrendered worldly desires, he resolved to brave all dangers and to risk his life for the only object for which he thought it worth while to live. He proceeded to the Yellow River, the Hoang-ho, and to the place where the caravans bound for India used to meet, and though the Governor had sent strict orders not to allow anyone to cross the frontier, the young priest, with the assistance of his co-religionists, succeeded in escaping the vigilance of the Chinese 'douaniers.' Spies were sent after him. But so frank was his avowal, and so firm his resolution, which he expressed in the presence of the authorities, that the Governor himself tore his hue-and-cry to pieces, and allowed him to proceed. Hitherto he had been accompanied by two friends. They now left him, and Hiouen-Thsang found himself alone, without a friend and without a guide. He sought for strength in fervent prayer. The next morning a person presented himself, offering his services as a guide. This guide conducted him safely for some distance, but left him when they approached the desert. There were still five watch-towers to be passed, and there was nothing to indicate the road through the desert, except the hoof-marks of horses, and skeletons. The traveller followed this melancholy track, and, though misled by the 'mirage' of the desert, he reached the first tower. Here the arrows of the watchmen would have put an end to his existence and his cherished expedition. But the officer in command, himself a zealous Buddhist, allowed the courageous pilgrim to proceed, and gave him letters of recommendation to the officers of the next towers. The last tower, however, was guarded by men inaccessible to bribes, and deaf to reasoning. In order to escape their notice, Hiouen-Thsang had to make a long *détour*. He passed through another desert, and lost his way. The bag in which he carried his water burst, and then even the courage of Hiouen-Thsang failed. He began to retrace his steps. But suddenly he stopped. 'I took an oath,' he said, 'never to make a step backward till I had reached India. Why, then, have I come here? It is better I should die proceeding to the West than return to the East and live.' Four nights and five days he travelled through the desert without a drop of water. He had nothing to refresh himself except his prayers—and what were they? Texts from a work which taught that there was no god, no Creator, no creation—nothing but mind, minding itself. It is incredible in how exhausted an atmosphere the divine spark within us will glimmer on, and even warm the dark chambers of the human heart. Comforted by his prayers, Hiouen-Thsang proceeded, and arrived after some time at a large lake. He was in the country of the Oigour Tatars. They received him well, nay, too well. One of the Tatar Khans, himself a Buddhist, sent for the Buddhist pilgrim, and insisted on his staying with him to instruct his people. Remonstrances proved of no avail. But Hiouen-Thsang was not to be conquered. 'I know,' he said, 'that the king, in spite of his power, has no power over my mind and my will;' and he refused all nourishment in order to put an end to his life. *Thanoumai kai eleutheresomai.* Three days he persevered, and at last the Khan, afraid of the consequences, was obliged to yield to the poor monk. He made him promise to visit him on his return to China, and then to stay three years with him. At last, after a delay of one month, during which the Khan and his Court came daily to hear the lessons of their pious guest, the traveller continued his journey with a numerous escort, and with letters of introduction from the Khan to twenty-four Princes whose territories the little caravan had to pass. Their way lay through what is now called Dsungaria, across the Musur-dabaghan mountains, the northern portion of the Belur-tag, the Yaxartes valley, Bactria, and Kabulistan. We cannot follow them through all the places they passed, though the accounts which he gives of their adventures are most interesting, and the description of the people most important. Here is a description of the Musur-dabaghan mountains :

'The top of the mountain rises to the sky. Since the beginning of the world the snow has been accumulating, and is now transformed into vast masses of ice, which never melt, either in spring or summer. Hard and brilliant sheets of snow are spread out till they are lost in the infinite, and mingle with the clouds. If one looks at them, the eyes are dazzled by the splendour. Frozen peaks hang down over both sides of the road, some hundred feet high, and twenty feet or thirty feet thick. It is not without difficulty and danger that the traveller can clear them or climb over them. Besides, there are squalls of wind and tornadoes of snow which attack the pilgrims. Even with double shoes, and in thick furs, one cannot help trembling and shivering.'

During the seven days that Hiouen-Thsang was crossing these Alpine passes he lost fourteen of his companions.

What is most important, however, in this early portion of the Chinese traveller is the account which he gives of the high degree of civilisation among the tribes of Central Asia. We had gradually accustomed ourselves to believe in an early civilisation of Egypt, of Babylon, of China, of India; but now that we find the hordes of Tatary possessing in the seventh century the chief arts and institutions of an advanced society, we shall soon have to drop the name of barbarians altogether. The theory of Oppert, who ascribes the original invention of the cuneiform letters and a civilisation anterior to that of Babylon and Nineveh to a Turanian or Scythian race, will lose much of its apparent improbability; for no new wave of civilisation had reached these countries between the cuneiform period of their literature and history and the time of Hiouen-Thsang's visit. In the kingdom of Okini, on the western frontier of China, Hiouen-Thsang found an active commerce, gold, silver, and copper coinage; monasteries, where the chief works of Buddhism were studied, and an alphabet, derived from Sanskrit. As he travelled on he met with mines, with agriculture, including pears, plums, peaches, almonds, grapes, pomegranates, rice, and wheat. The inhabitants were dressed in silk and woollen materials. There were musicians in the chief cities who played on the flute and the guitar. Buddhism was the prevailing religion, but there were traces of an earlier worship, the Bactrian fire-worship. The country was everywhere studded with halls, monasteries, monuments, and statues. Samarkand formed at that early time a kind of Athens, and its manners were copied by all the tribes in the neighbourhood. Balkh, the old capital of Bactria, was still an important place on the Oxus, well fortified, and full of sacred buildings. And the details which our traveller gives of the exact circumference of the cities, the number of their inhabitants, the products of the soil, the articles of trade, can leave no doubt in our minds that he relates what he had seen and heard himself. A new page in the history of the world is here opened, and new ruins pointed out, which would reward the pickaxe of a Layard.

But we must not linger. Our traveller, as we said, had entered India by way of Kabul. Shortly before he arrived at Pou-lou-cha-pou-lo, *i.e.* the Sanskrit Purushapura, the modern Peshawar, Hiouen-Thsang heard of an extraordinary cave where Buddha had formerly converted a dragon, and had promised his new pupil to leave him his shadow, in order that, whenever the evil passions of his dragon-nature should revive, the aspect of his master's shadowy features might remind him of his former vows. This promise was fulfilled, and the dragon-cave became a famous place of pilgrimage. Our traveller was told that the roads leading to the cave were extremely dangerous, and infested by robbers—that for three years none of the pilgrims had ever returned from the cave. But he replied, 'It would be difficult during a hundred thousand Kalpas to meet one single time with the true shadow of Buddha; how could I, having come so near, pass on without going to adore it?' He left his companions behind, and after asking in vain for a guide, he met at last with a boy who showed him to a farm belonging to a convent. Here he found an old man who undertook to act as his guide. They had hardly proceeded a few miles when they were attacked by five robbers. The monk took off his cap and displayed his ecclesiastical robes. 'Master,' said one of the robbers, 'where are you going?' Hiouen-Thsang replied, 'I desire to adore the shadow of Buddha.' 'Master,' said the robber, 'have you not heard that these roads are full of bandits?' 'Robbers are men,' Hiouen-Thsang exclaimed, 'and at present, when I am going to adore the shadow of Buddha, even though the roads were full of wild beasts, I should walk on without fear. Surely, then, I ought not to fear you, as you are men whose heart is possessed of pity.' The robbers were moved by these words, and opened their hearts to the true faith. After this little incident, Hiouen-Thsang proceeded with his guide. He passed a stream rushing down between two precipitous walls of rock. In the rock itself there was a door which opened. All was dark. But Hiouen-Thsang entered, advanced towards the east, then moved fifty steps backwards, and began his devotions. He made one hundred salutations, but he saw nothing. He reproached himself bitterly with his former sins, he cried, and abandoned himself to utter despair, because the shadow of Buddha would not appear before him. At last, after many prayers and invocations, he saw on the eastern wall a dim light, of the size of a saucepan, such as the Buddhist monks carry in their hands. But it disappeared. He continued praying full of joy and pain, and again he saw a light, which vanished like lightning. Then he vowed, full of devotion and love, that he would never leave the place till he had seen the shadow of the 'Venerable of the age.' After two hundred prayers, the cave was suddenly bathed in light, and the shadow of Buddha, of a brilliant white colour, rose majestically on the wall, as when the clouds suddenly open and all at once display the marvellous image of the 'Mountain of Light.' A dazzling splendour lighted up the features of the divine countenance. Hiouen-Thsang was lost in contemplation and wonder, and would not turn his eyes away from the sublime and incomparable object..... After he awoke from his trance, he called in six men, and commanded them to light a fire in the cave, in order to burn incense; but, as the approach of the light made the shadow of Buddha disappear, the fire was extinguished. Then five of the men saw the shadow, but the sixth saw nothing. The old man who had acted as guide was astounded when Hiouen-Thsang told him the vision. 'Master,' he said, 'without the sincerity of your faith, and the energy of your vows, you could not have seen such a miracle.'

This is the account given by Hiouen-Thsang's biographers. But we must say, to the credit of Hiouen-Thsang himself, that in the 'Si-yu-ki,' which contains his own diary, the story is told in a different way. The cave is described with almost the same words. But afterwards the writer continues : 'Formerly, the shadow of Buddha was seen in the cave, bright like his natural appearance, and with all the marks of his divine beauty. One might have said it was Buddha himself. For some centuries, however, it can no longer be seen completely. Though one does see something, it is only a feeble and doubtful resemblance. If a man prays with sincere faith, and if he has received from above a hidden impression, he sees the shadow clearly, but he cannot enjoy the sight for any length of time.'

From Peshawer, the scene of this extraordinary miracle, Hiouen-Thsang proceeded to Kashmir, visited the chief towns of Central India, and arrived at last in Magadha, the Holy Land of the Buddhists. Here he remained five years, devoting all his time to the study of Sanskrit and Buddhist literature, and inspecting every place hallowed by the recollections of the past. He then passed through Bengal, and proceeded to the south, with a view of visiting Ceylon, the chief seat of Buddhism. Baffled in that wish, he crossed the peninsula from east to west, ascended the Malabar Coast, reached the Indus, and after numerous excursions to the chief places of North-Western India, returned to Magadha, to spend there, with his old friends, some of the happiest years of his life. The route of his journeyings is laid down in a map drawn with exquisite skill by Vivien de Saint-Martin. At last Hiouen-Thsang was obliged to return to China, and, passing through the Penjab, Kabulistan, and Bactria, he reached the Oxus, followed its course nearly to its sources on the plateau of Pamir, and, after staying some time in the three chief towns of Turkistan, Khasgar, Yarkand, and Khoten, he found himself again, after sixteen years of travels, dangers, and studies, in his own native country. His fame had spread far and wide, and the poor pilgrim, who had once been hunted by imperial spies and armed policemen, was now received with public honours by the Emperor himself. His entry into the capital was like a triumph. The streets were covered with carpets, flowers were scattered, and banners flying. Soldiers were drawn up, the magistrates went out to meet him, and all the monks of the neighbourhood marched along in solemn procession. The trophies that adorned this triumph, carried by a large number of horses, were of a peculiar kind. First, 150 grains of the dust of Buddha; secondly, a golden statue of the great Teacher; thirdly, a similar statue of sandal-wood; fourthly, a statue of sandal-wood, representing Buddha as descending from heaven; fifthly, a statue of silver; sixthly, a golden statue of Buddha conquering the dragons; seventhly, a statue of sandal-wood, representing Buddha as a preacher; lastly, a collection of 657 works in 520 volumes. The Emperor received the traveller in the Phœnix Palace, and, full of admiration for his talents and wisdom, invited him to accept a high office in the Government. This Hiouen-Thsang declined. 'The soul of the administration,' he said, 'is still the doctrine of Confucius;' and he would dedicate the rest of his life to the Law of Buddha. The Emperor thereupon asked him to write an account of his travels and assigned him a monastery where he might employ his leisure in translating the works he had brought back from India. His travels were soon written and published, but the translation of the Sanskrit MSS. occupied all the remaining years of his life. It is said that the number of works translated by him, with the assistance of a large staff of monks, amounted to 740, in 1,335 volumes. Frequently he might be seen meditating on a difficult passage, when suddenly it seemed as if a higher spirit had enlightened his mind. His soul was cheered, as when a man walking in darkness sees all at once the sun piercing the clouds and shining in its full brightness; and, unwilling to trust to his own understanding, he used to attribute his knowledge to a secret inspiration of Buddha and the Bodhisattvas. When he found that the hour of death approached, he had all his property divided among the poor. He invited his friends to come and see him, and to take a cheerful leave of that impure body of Hiouen-Thsang. 'I desire,' he said, 'that whatever rewards I may have merited by good works may fall upon other people. May I be born again with them in the heaven of the blessed, be admitted to the family of Mi-le, and serve the Buddha of the future, who is full of kindness and affection. When I descend again upon earth to pass through other forms of existence, I desire at every new birth to fulfil my duties towards Buddha, and arrive at the last at the highest and most perfect intelligence.' He died in the year 664—about the same time that Mohammedanism was pursuing its bloody conquests in the East, and Christianity began to shed its pure light over the dark forests of Germany.

It is impossible to do justice to the character of so extraordinary a man as Hiouen-Thsang in so short a sketch as we have been able to give. If we knew only his own account of his life and travels—the volume which has just been published at Paris—we should be ignorant of the motives which guided him and of the sufferings which he underwent. Happily, two of his friends and pupils have left an account of their teacher, and Stanislas Julien has acted wisely in beginning his collection of the Buddhist Pilgrims with the translation of that biography. There we learn something of the man himself and of that silent enthusiasm which supported him in his arduous work. There we see him braving the dangers of the desert, scrambling along glaciers, crossing over torrents, and quietly submitting to the brutal violence of Indian Thugs. There we see him rejecting the tempting invitations of Khans, Kings, and Emperors, and quietly pursuing among strangers, within the bleak walls of the cell of a Buddhist college, the study of a foreign language, the key to the sacred literature of his faith. There we see him rising to eminence, acknowledged as an equal by his former teachers, as a superior by the most distinguished scholars of India; the champion of the orthodox faith, an arbiter at councils, the favourite of Indian kings. In his own work there is hardly a word about all this. We do not wish to disguise his weaknesses, such as they appear in the same biography. He was a credulous man, easily imposed upon by crafty priests, still more easily carried away by his own superstitions; but he deserved to have lived in better times, and we almost grudge so high and noble a character to a country not our own, and to a religion unworthy of such a man. Of selfishness we find no trace in him. His whole life belonged to the faith in which he was born, and the object of his labour was not so much to perfect himself as to benefit others. He was an honest man. And strange, and stiff, and absurd, and outlandish as his outward appearance may seem, there is something in the face of that poor Chinese monk, with his yellow skin and his small oblique eyes, that appeals to our sympathy—something in his life, and the work of his life, that places him by right among the heroes of Greece, the martyrs of Rome, the knights of the crusades, the explorers of the Arctic regions—something that makes us feel it a duty to inscribe his name on the roll of the 'forgotten worthies' of the human race. There is a higher consanguinity than that of the blood which runs through our veins—that of the blood which makes our hearts beat with the same indignation and the same joy. And there is a higher nationality than that of being governed by the same imperial dynasty—that of our common allegiance to the Father and Ruler of all mankind.

CHAPTER III

THE MEANING OF NIRVANA

Even in one and the same school we find different parties maintaining different views on the meaning of Nirvana. There is the school of the Svabhavikas, which still exists in Nepal. The Svabhavikas maintain that nothing exists but nature, or rather substance, and that this substance exists by itself (svabhavat), without a Creator or a Ruler. It exists, however, under two forms : in the state of Pravritti, as active, or in the state of Nirvritti, as passive. Human beings, who, like everything else, exist svabhavat, 'by themselves,' are supposed to be capable of arriving at Nirvritti, or passiveness, which is nearly synonymous with Nirvana. But here the Svabhavikas branch off into two sects. Some believe that Nirvritti is repose, others that it is annihilation; and the former add, 'were it even annihilation (sunyata), it would still be good, man being otherwise doomed to an eternal migration through all the forms of nature; the more desirable of which are little to be wished for; and the less so, at any price to be shunned.'[1]

What was the original meaning of Nirvana may perhaps best be seen from the etymology of this technical term. Every Sanskrit scholar knows that Nirvana means originally the blowing out, the extinction of light, and not absorption. The human soul, when it arrives at its perfection, is blown out,[2] if we use the phraseology of the Buddhists, like a lamp; it is not absorbed, as the Brahmans say, like a drop in the ocean. Neither in the system of Buddhist philosophy, nor in the philosophy from which Buddha is supposed to have borrowed, was there any place left for a Divine Being; and if there is no Divine Being, into what can the human soul be absorbed ? Sankhya philosophy, in its original form, claims the name of an-isvara, 'lordless' or 'atheistic,' as its distinctive title. Its final object is not absorption in God,

[1] See Burnouf, *Introduction*, p. 441; Hodgson, *Asiatic Researches*, vol. xvi.

[2] 'Calm,' 'without wind,' as Nirvana is sometimes explained, is expressed in Sanskrit by Nirvata. See Amara-Kosha, *sub voce*.

whether personal or impersonal, but Moksha, deliverance of the soul from all pain and illusion, and recovery by the soul of its true nature—possibly, a return to the true self. It is doubtful whether the term Nirvana was coined by Buddha. It occurs in the literature of the Brahmans as a synonym of Moksha, deliverance; Nirvritti, cessation; Apavarga, release; Nihsreyas, *summum bonum*. It is used in this sense in the Mahabharata, and it is explained in the Amara-Koṣha as having the meaning of 'blowing out, applied to a fire and to a sage.'[3] Unless, however, we succeed in tracing this term in works which can be proved to be anterior to Buddha, we may admit that it was invented by him in order to express that meaning of the *summum bonum* which he was the first to preach, and which some of his disciples explained in the sense of absolute annihilation.

The earliest authority to which we can go back, if we want to know the original character of Buddhism, is the Buddhist Canon, as settled after the death of Buddha at the first Council. It is called Tripitaka, or the Three Baskets, the first containing the Sutras, or the discourses of Buddha; the second, the Vinaya, or his code of morality; the third, the Abhidharma, or the system of metaphysics. The first was compiled by Ananda, the second by Upali, the third by Kasyapa—all of them the pupils and friends of Buddha. It may be that these collections, as we now possess them, were finally arranged, not at the first, but at the third Council. Yet, even then, we have no earlier, no more authentic, documents from which we could form an opinion as to the original teaching of Buddha; and the Nirvana, as taught both in the metaphysics of Kasyapa and in the Prajna-paramita of the Northern Buddhists, is annihilation, not absorption. Buddhism, therefore, if tested by its own canonical books, cannot be freed from the charge of Nihilism, whatever may have been its character in the mind of its founder, and whatever changes it may have undergone in later times, and among races less inured to metaphysical discussions than the Hindus.

[3] Different views of the Nirvana, as conceived by the Tirthakas, or the Brahmans, may be seen in an extract from the Lankavatara, translated by Burnouf, p. 514.

The ineradicable feeling of dependence on something else, which is the life-spring of all religion, was completely numbed in the early Buddhist metaphysicians, and it was only after several generations had passed away, and after Buddhism had become the creed of millions, that this feeling returned with increased warmth, changing, as I said in my article, the very Nothing into a paradise, and deifying the very Buddha who had denied the existence of a Deity. That this has been the case in China we know from the interesting works of the Abbe Huc, and from other sources, such as the 'Catechism of the Shamans, or the Laws and Regulations of the Priesthood of Buddha in China,' translated by Ch. F. Neumann, London, 1831. In India, also, Buddhism, as soon as it became a popular religion, had to speak a more human language than that of metaphysical Pyrrhonism. But, if it did so, it was because it was shamed into it. This we may see from the very nicknames which the Brahmans apply to their opponents, the Bauddhas. They call them Nastikas—those who maintain that there is nothing; Sunyavadins—those who maintain that there is a universal void.

The only ground, therefore, on which we may stand, if we wish to defend the founder of Buddhism against the charges of Nihilism and Atheism, is this, that, as some of the Buddhists admit, the 'Basket of Metaphysics' was rather the work of his pupils, not of Buddha himself.[4] This distinction between the authentic words of Buddha and the canonical books in general is mentioned more than once. The priesthood of Ceylon, when the manifest errors with which their canonical commentaries abound were brought to their notice, retreated from their former position, and now assert that it is only the express words of Buddha that they receive as undoubted truth.[5] There is a passage in a Buddhist work which reminds us somewhat of the last page

[4] See Burnouf, *Introduction*, p. 41. Abuddhoktam abhidharmasastram. *Ibid.*, p. 454. According to the Tibetan Buddhists, however, Buddha propounded the Abhidharma when he was fifty-one years old. *Asiatic Researches*, vol. xx, p. 339.

[5] *Eastern Monachism*, p. 171.

of Dean Milman's 'History of Christianity,' and where we read :

'The words of the priesthood are good; those of the Rahats (saints) are better; but those of the All-knowing are the best of all.'

This is an argument which Francis Barham might have used with more success, and by which he might have justified, if not the first disciples, at least the original founder of Buddhism. Nay, there is a saying of Buddha's which tends to show that all metaphysical discussion was regarded by him as vain and useless. It is a saying mentioned in one of the MSS. belonging to the Bodleian Library. As it has never been published before, I may be allowed to quote it in the original : Sadasad vicharam na sahate—'The ideas of being and not being do not admit of discussion'—a tenet which, if we consider that it was enunciated before the time of the Eleatic philosophers of Greece, and long before Hegel's Logic, might certainly have saved us many an intricate and indigestible argument.

A few passages from the Buddhist writings of Nepal and Ceylon will best show that the *horror nihili* was not felt by the metaphysicians of former ages in the same degree as it is felt by ourselves. The famous hymn which resounds in heaven when the luminous rays of the smile of Buddha penetrate through the clouds, is 'All is transitory, all is misery, all is void, all is without substance.' Again, it is said in the Prajna-paramita[6] that Buddha began to think that he ought to conduct all creatures to perfect Nirvana. But he reflected that there are really no creatures which ought to be conducted, nor creatures that conduct; and, nevertheless, he did conduct all creatures to perfect Nirvana. Then, continues the text, why is it said that there are neither creatures which arrive at complete Nirvana, nor creatures which conduct there ? Because it is illusion which makes creatures what they are. It is as if a clever juggler, or his pupil, made an immense number of people to appear on the high road, and after having made them to appear, made them to disappear again. Would there be anybody who had killed, or murdered, or annihilated, or caused them to vanish ? No. And it is the same with Buddha. He conducts an immense, innumerable, infinite number of

[6] Burnouf, *Introduction*, p. 462.

creatures to complete Nirvana, and yet there are neither creatures which are conducted, nor creatures that conduct. If a Bodhisattva, on hearing this explanation of the Law, is not frightened, then it may be said that he has put on the great armour.[7]

Soon after, we read : 'The name of Buddha is nothing but a word. The name of Bodhisattva is nothing but a word. The name of Perfect Wisdom (Prajna-paramita) is nothing but a word. The name is indefinite, as if one says "I," for "I" is something indefinite, because it has no limits.'

Burnouf gives the gist of the whole Prajna-paramita in the following words : 'The highest Wisdom, or what is to be known, has no more real existence than he who has to know, or the Bodhisattva; no more than he who does know, or the Buddha.' But Burnouf remarks that nothing of this kind is to be found in the Sutras, and that Gautama Sakyamuni, the son of Suddhodana, would never have become the founder of a popular religion if he had started with similar absurdities. In the Sutras the reality of the objective world is denied; the reality of form is denied; the reality of the individual, or the 'I,' is equally denied. But the existence of a subject, of something like the Purusha, the thinking substance of the Sankhya philosophy, is spared. Something at least exists with respect to which everything else may be said not to exist. The germs of the ideas, developed in the Prajna-paramita, may indeed be discovered here and there in the Sutras also.[8] But they had not yet ripened into that poisonous plant which soon became an indispensable narcotic in the schools of the later Buddhists. Buddha himself, however, though, perhaps, not a Nihilist, was certainly an Atheist. He does not deny distinctly either the existence of gods, or that of God; but he ignores the former, and he is ignorant of the latter. Therefore, if Nirvana in his mind was not yet complete annihilation, still less could it have been absorption into a Divine essence. It was nothing but self-ness, in the metaphysical sense of the word—a relapse into that being which is nothing but itself. This is the most charitable view which we can take of the Nirvana, even as conceived by Buddha himself, and it is this view which Burnouf derived

[7] Burnouf, *Introduction*, p. 478.

[8] *Ibid.*, p. 520.

from the canonical books of the Northern Buddhists. Spence Hardy, who in his works follows exclusively the authority of the Southern Buddhists, the Pali and Singhalese works of Ceylon, arrives at the same result. We read in his work : 'The Rahat (Arhat), who has reached Nirvana, but is not yet a Pratyeka-buddha, or a Supreme Budda, says : "I await the appointed time for the cessation of existence. I have no wish to live; I have no wish to die. Desire is extinct."'

In a very interesting dialogue between Milinda and Nagasena, communicated by Spence Hardy, Nirvana is represented as something which has no antecedent cause, no qualities, no locality. It is something of which the utmost we may assert is, that it is.

Nagasena : Can a man, by his natural strength, go from the city of Sagal to the forest of Himala?

Milinda : Yes.

Nagasena : But could any man, by his natural strength, bring the forest of Himala to this city of Sagal ?

Milinda : No.

Nagasena : In like manner, though the fruition of the paths may cause the accomplishment of Nirvana, no cause by which Nirvana is produced can be declared. The path that leads to Nirvana may be pointed out, but not any cause for its production. Why ? Because that which constitutes Nirvana is beyond all computation—a mystery, not to be understood.... It cannot be said that it is produced, nor that it is not produced; that it is past or future or present. Nor can it be said that it is the seeing of the eye, or the hearing of the ear, or the smelling of the nose, or the tasting of the tongue, or the feeling of the body.

Milinda : Then you speak of a thing that is not; you merely say that Nirvana is Nirvana;—therefore there is no Nirvana.

Nagasena : Great king, Nirvana is.

Another question also, whether Nirvana is something different from the beings that enter into it, has been asked by the Buddhists themselves :

Milinda : Does the being who acquires it, attain something that has previously existed ?—or is it his own product, a formation peculiar to himself ?

Nagasena : Nirvana does not exist previously to its reception; nor is it that which was brought into existence. Still to the being who attains it, there is Nirvana.

In opposition, therefore, to the more advanced views of the Nihilistic philosophers of the North, Nagasena maintains the existence of Nirvana, and of the being that has entered Nirvana. He does not say that Buddha is a mere word. When asked by King Milinda, whether the all-wise Buddha exists, he replies :

Nagasena : He who is the most meritorious (Bhagavat) does exist.

Milinda : Then can you point out to me the place in which he exists ?

Nagasena : Our Bhagavat has attained Nirvana, where there is no repetition of birth. We cannot say that he is here or that he is there. When a fire is extinguished, can it be said that it is here or that it is there ? Even so our Buddha has attained extinction (Nirvana). He is like the sun that has set behind the Astagiri mountain. It cannot be said that he is here or that he is there : but we can point him out by the discourses he delivered. In them he lives.

At the present moment, the great majority of Buddhists would probably be quite incapable of understanding the abstract speculation of their ancient masters, and the view taken of Nirvana in China, Mongolia, and Tatary may hardly be less gross than that which most of the Mohammedans form of their paradise. But in the history of religion, the historian must go back to the earliest and most original documents that are to be obtained. Thus only may he hope to understand the later developments which, whether for good or evil, every form of faith has had to undergo.

CHAPTER IV

BUDDHIST NIHILISM

Buddhism, in its numerous varieties, still continues the religion of the majority of mankind, and will therefore always occupy a very prominent place in a comparative study of the religions of the world. And comparative theology, although the youngest branch on the tree of human knowledge, will, for an accurate and fruitful study of antiquity, soon become as indispensable as comparative philology. For how can we truly understand and properly appreciate a people, its literature, art, politics, morals and philosophy, its entire conception of life, without having comprehended its religion, not only in its outer aspect, but in its innermost being, in its deepest far-reaching roots ?

What our great poet once said almost prophetically of languages, may also be said of religions—'*He who knows only one, knows none.*' As the true knowledge of a language requires a knowledge of languages, a true knowledge of religion requires a knowledge of religions. And though the assertion that all the languages of mankind are Oriental may sound too bold, true it is that all religions, like the sun, have risen from the East.

Here, therefore, in treating religions scientifically (those of the Aryan as well as those of the Semitic races) the Oriental scholar lawfully enters into what you call the 'plenum' of philology, if philology still is, what it once intended and wished to be, viz. the true Humanitas, which, like an Emperor of yore, could say of itself, 'humani nihil a me alienum puto.' ('I consider nothing which is human as alien to myself.')

Now, it has been the peculiar fate of the religion of Buddha that among all the so-called false or heathenish religions, it almost alone has been praised by all and everybody for its elevated, pure, and humanising character. One hardly trusts one's eyes on seeing Catholic and Protestant missionaries vie with each other in their praises of the Buddha; and even the attention of those who are indifferent to all that concerns religion must be arrested for a moment when they learn from statistical accounts that no religion, not even the Christian, has exercised so powerful an influence on the diminution of crime as the old simple doctrine of the Ascetic of Kapilavastu. Indeed, no better authority can be brought forward in this respect than that of a still living Bishop of the Roman Catholic Church. In his interesting work on the life of Buddha, the author, the Bishop of Ramatha, the Vicar Apostolic of Ava and Pegu, speaks with so much candour of the merits of the Buddhist religion that we are often at a loss which most to admire, his courage or his learning. Thus he says in one place[1]: 'There are many moral precepts equally commanded and enforced in common by both creeds. It will not be deemed rash to assert that most of the moral truths prescribed by the Gospel, are to be met with in the Buddhistic scriptures.' In another place Bishop Bigandet says[2]: 'In reading the particulars of the life of the last Budha Gaudama, it is impossible not to feel reminded of many circumstances relating to our Saviour's life, such as it has been sketched out by the Evangelists.'

I might produce many even stronger testimonies in honour of Buddha and Buddhism, but the above suffice for my purpose.

But then, on the other hand, it seems as if people had only permitted themselves to be so liberal in their praises of Buddha and Buddhism because they could, in the end, condemn a religion which, in spite of all its merits, culminated in Atheism and Nihilism. Thus we are told by Bishop Bigandet[3]: 'It may be said in favour of Buddhism that no philosophico-religious system has ever upheld, to an equal degree, the notions of a saviour and deliverer, and the necessity of his mission for procuring the salvation of man, in a Buddhist sense. The *rôle* of Buddha, from beginning to end, is that of a deliverer, who preaches a law designed to secure to man the deliverance from all the miseries he is labouring under. But by an inexplicable and deplorable eccentricity, the pretended saviour, after having taught man the way to deliver himself from the tyranny of his passions, leads him, after all, into the bottomless gulf of a total annihilation.'

[1] Page 494. [2] Page 495. [3] Page viii.

This language may have a slightly episcopal tinge, yet we find the same judgment, in almost identical words, pronounced by the most eminent scholars who have written on Buddhism. The warm discussions on this subject which have recently taken place at the *Academie des Inscriptions et Belles-Lettres* of Paris are probably known to many . . . ; but better still, the work of the man whose place has not yet been filled, either in the French Academy, or at the Council Board of German Science—the work of Eugene Burnouf, the true founder of a scientific study of Buddhism. Burnouf, too, in his researches arrives at the same result, viz.: that Buddhism, as known to us from its canonical books, in spite of its great qualities, ends in Atheism and Nihilism.

Now, as to Atheism, it cannot be denied that, if we call the old gods of the Veda—Indra, and Agni, and Yama—gods, Buddha was an Atheist. He does not believe in the divinity of these deities. What is noteworthy is that he does not by any means deny their bare existence, just as little as St. Augustine and other fathers of the Church endeavoured to sublimise or entirely to explain away the existence of the Olympian deities. The founder of Buddhism treats the old gods as superhuman beings, and promises the believers that they shall after death be reborn into the world of the gods, and shall enjoy divine bliss with the blessed gods. Similarly he threatens the wicked that after death they shall meet with their punishment in the subterranean abodes and hells, where the Asuras, Sarpas, Nagas, and other evil spirits dwell, beings whose existence was more firmly rooted in the popular belief and language than that even the founder of a new religion could have dared to reason them away. But, although Buddha assigned to these mediatised gods and devils, palaces, gardens, and a court, not second to their former ones, he yet deprived them of all their sovereign rights. Although, according to Buddha, the worlds of the gods last for millions of years, they must perish, at the end of every kalpa, with the gods and with the spirits who in the circle of births have raised themselves to the world of the gods. Indeed, the reorganisation of the spirit-world goes further still. Already, before Buddha, the Brahmans had surmounted the low standpoint of mythological polytheism, and supplanted it by the idea of the Brahman, as the absolute divine or super-divine power. What, then, does Buddha decree ? To this Brahman also he assigns a place in his universe. Over and above the world of the gods with its six paradises he heaps up sixteen Brahma-worlds, not to be attained through virtue and piety only, but through inner contemplation, through knowledge and enlightenment. The dwellers in these worlds are already purely spiritualised beings, without body, without weight, without desire, far above men and gods. Indeed, the Buddhist architect rises to a still more towering height, heaping upon the Brahma-world four still higher worlds, which he calls the world of the formless. All these worlds are open to man, and the beings ascend and descend in the circle of time, according to the works they have performed, according to the truths they have recognised. But in all these worlds the law of change obtains; in none is there exemption from birth, age, and death. The world of the gods will perish like that of men, even the world of the formless will not last for ever; but the Buddha, the Enlightened and truly Free, stands higher, and will not be affected or disturbed by the collapse of the Universe : 'Si fractus illabatur orbis, impavidum ferient ruinæ.'

Now, however, we meet with a vein of irony, which one would hardly have expected in Buddha. Gods and devils he had located; to all mythological and philosophical acquisitions of the past he had done justice as far as possible. Even fabulous beings, such as Nagas, Gandharvas, and Garudas, had escaped the process of dissolution which was to reach them later only at the hands of comparative mythology. There is only *one* idea, the idea of a personal creator, in regard to which Buddha is relentless.

It is not only denied, but even its origin, like that of an ancient myth, is carefully explained in its minutest details. This is done in the Brahmajalasutra. Let us bear in mind that a destruction of the worlds occurs at the end of every kalpa, a destruction which not only annihilates earth and hell, but also all the worlds of the gods, and even the three lowest of the Brahma-worlds. A description of the duration of a kalpa can only be given in the language of Buddhism. Take a rock forming a cube of about fourteen miles, touch it once in a hundred years with a piece of fine cloth, and the rock will sooner be reduced to dust than a kalpa will have attained its end. It is said that at the end of the kalpa, after all the lower stories of the universe had been destroyed and a new world had again been slowly formed, the spirits dwelling in the higher Brahma-worlds had remained inviolate. Then one of these spirits, a being without body, without weight, omnipresent and blessed within himself, descended, when his time had arrived, from the higher Brahma-world to the new-formed nether Brahma-world. There he first dwelt alone; but, by and by, the desire arose in him not to remain alone any longer. At the moment of the awakening of this desire within him, a second being accidentally descended from the higher into the lower Brahma-world. Then and there the thought originated in the first being, 'I am the Brahma, the great Brahma, the Highest, the Unconquerable, the Omniscient, the Lord and King of All. I am the Creator of all things, the Father of All. *This* being has also been created by me; for as soon as I desired not to remain alone, my desire brought forth this second being.' The other beings as they gradually descended from the higher worlds likewise believed that the first comer had been their Creator, for was he not older and mightier and handsomer than they?

But this is not all; for although it would explain how one spirit could consider himself the creator of other spirits, it would leave unexplained the circumstances of men on earth believing in such a creator. This is explained in the following manner: 'In the course of time one of these higher beings sank lower and lower, and was finally born as a man on earth. There, by penances and deep meditations, he attained a state of inner enlightenment, which gives to man the faculty of remembering his former existences. He remembered the above-narrated occurrences in the newly-originated Brahma-world, and announced to mankind that there was a Creator, a Brahman, who had been prior to all other beings; that this Creator was eternal and immutable, while all beings created by him were mutable and mortal.'

There is in this explanation, I believe, an unmistakeable note of animosity, otherwise so alien to the character of Buddha, and the question naturally arises whether this can have been the doctrine of the founder of Buddhism himself. And herewith we at once approach our principal problem— *Is it possible to distinguish between Buddhism and the personal teaching of Buddha?'* We possess the Buddhist canon and have a right to consider all that we find in this canon as orthodox Buddhist doctrine. But as there has been no lack of efforts in Christian theology to distinguish between the doctrine of the founder of our religion and that of the writers of the Gospels, to go beyond the canon of the New Testament, and to make the *logia* of the Master the only valid rule of our faith, so a similar want was felt at a very early period among the followers of Buddha. King Asoka, the Indian Constantine, had to remind the assembled priests at the great Council which had to settle the Buddhist canon, *that what had been said by Buddha, that alone was well said.*[4] Works attributed to Buddha, but declared as apocryphal, or even as heterodox, already existed at that time.

Thus we are not by any means without an authority for distinguishing between Buddhism and the teaching of Buddha; the question is only whether such a separation is still practicable for us?

My belief is that all honest enquirers must oppose a No to this question. Burnouf never ventured to cast a glance beyond the boundaries of the Buddhist canon. What he finds in the canonical books, in the so-called 'Three Baskets,' is to him the doctrine of Buddha, similarly as we must accept, as the doctrine of Christ, what is contained in the four Gospels.

Still the question ought to be asked again and again, whether, at least with regard to certain doctrines or facts, it may not be possible to make a step further in advance, even with the conviction that it cannot lead us to results of apodictic certainty. For if, as happens frequently, we find in the different parts of the canon, views, not only differing from, but even contradictory to each other, it follows, I think, that one only of them can belong to Buddha personally, and I believe that in such a case we have the right to choose, and the liberty to accept *that* view as the original one, the one peculiar to Buddha, which *least* harmonises with the later system of orthodox Buddhism.

As regards the denial of a Creator, or Atheism in the ordinary acceptation of the term, I do not think that any

See *Selected Essays*, vol. i, p. 17.

one passage from the books of the canon known to us can be quoted which contradicts it, or which in any way presupposes the belief in a personal God or a Creator. All that may be urged are the words said to have been spoken by Buddha at the moment when he became the Enlightened, the Buddha. They are as follows: 'Looking for the maker of this tabernacle, I shall have to run through a course of many births, as long as I do not find (him);—and painful is birth again and again. But now, maker of the tabernacle, thou hast been seen; thou shalt not make up this tabernacle again. All thy rafters are broken, thy ridge-pole is sundered; the mind, approaching the Eternal (Nirvana), has attained to the extinction of all desires."[5]

Here in the maker of the tabernacle, **i.e.** of the body, one might be tempted to see a creator. But he who is acquainted with the general direction of thought in Buddhism, soon finds that this architect of the house is only a poetical expression, and that whatever meaning may underlie it, it evidently signifies a force subordinated to the Buddha, the Enlightened. Buddha had conquered Mara, the representative of worldly temptations, the father of all worldly desires; and as desire is indirectly the cause of birth, the destruction of desire and the conquest of Mara are nearly the same thing.

But whilst we have no ground for exonerating the Buddha personally from the accusation of Atheism, the matter stands very differently as regards the charge of Nihilism. Buddhist Nihilism has always been much more incomprehensible than mere Atheism. A kind of religion is still conceivable, when there is something firm somewhere, when a something, eternal and self-dependent, is recognised, if not *without* and *above* man, at least *within* him. But if, as Buddhism teaches, the soul after having passed through all the phases of existence, through all the worlds of the gods and of the higher spirits, attains finally Nirvana as its highest aim and last reward, *i.e.* becomes quite extinct, then religion is not any more what it ought to be—a bridge from the finite to the infinite, but a trap-bridge hurling man into the abyss at the very moment when he thought he had arrived at the stronghold of the Eternal. According to the metaphysical doctrine of Buddhism, the soul cannot dissolve

[5] Dhammapada, *v.* 153.

itself in a higher being, or be absorbed in an absolute substance, as was taught by the Brahmans and other mystics of ancient and modern times. For Buddhism knew not the Divine, the Eternal, the Absolute, and the soul, even as the I, or as the mere Self, the Atman, as called by the Brahmans, was represented in the orthodox metaphysics of Buddhism as transient, as futile, as a mere phantom.

No person who reads with attention the metaphysical speculations on the Nirvana contained in the Buddhist canon, can arrive at any conviction different from that expressed by Burnouf, *viz.* : That Nirvana, the highest aim, the *summum bonum* of Buddhism, is the absolute nothing.

Burnouf adds, however, that this doctrine, in its crude form, appears only in the third part of the canon, the so-called Abhidharma, but not in the first and second parts, in the Sutras, the sermons, and the Vinaya, the ethics, which together bear the name of Dharma or Law. He next points out that, according to some ancient authorities, this entire part of the canon was designated as 'not pronounced by Buddha.'[6] These are, at once, two important limitations. I add a third, and maintain that sayings of the Buddha occur in the first and second parts of the canon, which are in open contradiction to this metaphysical Nihilism.

Now, as regards the soul, or the self, the existence of which, according to the orthodox metaphysics, is purely phenomenal, a sentence attributed to the Buddha says[7] : 'Self is the Lord of Self; who else could be the Lord ?' And again[8], 'A man who controls himself enters the untrodden land through his own self-controlled self.' And this untrodden land is the Nirvana.

Nirvana certainly means extinction, whatever its later arbitrary interpretations may have been, and seems, therefore, to imply, even etymologically, a real blowing out or passing away. But Nirvana occurs also in the Brahmanic writings, as synonymous with Moksha, Nirvritti, and other words, all designating the highest stage of spiritual liberty and bliss, but not annihilation. Nirvana may mean the extinction of many things—of selfishness, desire, and sin,

[6] M. M.'s *Selected Essays*. The later origin of the Abhidharma was denied by D'Alwis in his Essay on Nirvana, and defended by Oldenberg, *Vinaya*, vol. i, p. xi.

[7] Dhammapada, *v.* 160.

[8] *Ibid., v.* 323.

without going so far as the extinction of being and self-consciousness. Further, if we consider that Buddha himself, after he had already seen Nirvana, still remains on earth until his body falls a prey to death; that Buddha appears, in the legends, to his disciples even after his death,[9] it seems to me that all these circumstances are hardly reconcilable with the orthodox metaphysical doctrine of Nirvana.

What does it mean when Buddha[10] calls earnestness the path of immortality, and thoughtlessness the path of death? Buddhaghosha, a learned man of the fifth century, here explains immortality by Nirvana, and that this was also Buddha's thought is clearly established by a passage following immediately after[11] : 'These wise people, meditative, steady, always possessed of strong powers, attain to Nirvana, the highest happiness.' Can this be annihilation? And would such expressions have been used by the founder of this new religion, if what he called immortality had, in his own idea, been annihilation?

I could quote many more such passages did I not fear to tire you. Nirvana occurs even in the purely moral sense of quietness and absence of passion. 'When a man can bear everything without uttering a sound,' says Buddha[12] 'he has attained Nirvana.' Quiet long-suffering he calls the highest Nirvana[13]; he who has conquered passion and hatred is said to enter into Nirvana.[14]

In other passages, Nirvana is described as the result of just knowledge. Thus we read[15] : 'Hunger or desire is the worst of diseases, the body the greatest of pains; if one knows this truly, that is Nirvana, the highest happiness.'

When it is said in one passage that rest (Santi) is the highest bliss[16], it is said in another that Nirvana is the highest bliss.

Buddha says[17] : 'The sages who injure nobody, and who always control their body, they will go to the unchangeable place (Nirvana), where, if they have gone, they will suffer no more.'

[9] See *supra*.
[10] Dhammapada, *v.* 21.
[11] *Ibid.*, *v.* 23.
[12] Dhammapada, *v.* 134.
[13] *Ibid.*, *v.* 184.
[14] *Ibid.*, *v.* 369.
[15] Dhammapada, *v.* 203.
[16] *Ibid.*, *v.* 285.
[17] *Ibid.*, *v.* 225.

Nirvana is called the quiet place,[18] the immortal place,[19] even simply *that* which is immortal[20]; and the expression occurs,[21] that the wise dive into this immortal. As, according to Buddha, everything that was made, everything that was put together, passes away again, and resolves itself into its component parts, he calls in contradistinction that which is not made, *i.e.*, the uncreated and eternal, Nirvana.[22] He says[23] : 'When you have understood the destruction of all that was made, you will understand that which was not made.' Whence it appears that even for him a certain something exists, which is not made, which is eternal and imperishable.

On considering such sayings, to which many more might be added, one recognises in them a conception of Nirvana, altogether irreconcilable with the Nihilism of the third part of the Buddhist Canon. The question in such matters is not a more or less, but an *aut-aut*. If these sayings have maintained themselves, in spite of their contradiction to orthodox metaphysics, the only explanation, in my opinion, is that they were too firmly fixed in the tradition which went back to Buddha and his disciples. What Bishop Bigandet and others represent as the popular view of the Nirvana, in contradistinction to that of the Buddhist divines, was, if I am not mistaken, the conception of Buddha and his disciples. It represented the entrance of the soul into rest, a subduing of all wishes and desires, indifference to joy and pain, to good and evil, an absorption of the soul in itself, and a freedom from the circle of existences from birth to death, and from death to a new birth. This is still the meaning which educated people attach to it, whilst to the minds of the larger masses[24] Nirvana suggests rather the idea of a Mohammedan paradise or of blissful Elysian fields.

[18] Dhammapada, *vv.* 368, 381. [20] Dhammapada, *v.* 374. [22] Dhammapada, *v.* 97.
[19] *Ibid.*, *v.* 114. [21] *Ibid.*, *v.* 411. [23] *Ibid.*, *v.* 383.

[24] Bigandet.—*The Life or Legend of Gaudama, the Buddha of the Burmese*, with Annotations. The Ways to Neibban, and Notice on the Phongyies, or Burmese Monks. Pp. xi, 538. Bastian, *Die Völker des östlichen Asien*, vol. iii, p. 353.

Only in the hands of the philosophers, to whom Buddhism owes its metaphysics, the Nirvana, through constant negations, carried to an indefinite degree, through the excluding and abstracting of all that is not Nirvana, at last became an empty Nothing, a philosophical myth. There is no lack of such philosophical myths either in the East or in the West. What has been fabled by philosophers of a Nothing, and of the terrors of a Nothing, is as much a myth as the myth of Eos and Tithonus. There is no more a Nothing than there is an Eos or a Chaos. All these are sickly, dying, or dead words, which, like shadows and ghosts, continue to haunt language, and succeed in deceiving for a while even the healthiest understanding.

Even modern philosophy is not afraid to say that there is a Nothing. We find passages in the German mystics, such as Eckhart and Tauler, where the abyss of the Nothing is spoken of quite in a Buddhist style.[25] If Buddha had said, like St. Paul, 'that what no eye hath seen, nor ear heard, neither has it entered into the heart of man,' was prepared in the Nirvana for those who had advanced to the highest degree of spiritual perfection, such expressions would have

[25] About the same time when this deeply religious Nihilism found expression in Germany in the works of Eckhart and Tauler, it shows itself in Wales also. In a letter which I received from the author of the *Literature of the Kymry*, Thomas Stephens sends me the following specimen, taken from the *Myvyrian Archæology*, vol. iii, p. 34 :

No Secret but No-thing,
No-thing but the Infinite,
No Infinite but God,
No God but No-thing,
No-thing but (the) Secret,
No Secret but God.

The thought evidently is, that all *things* are perishable, but that the Infinite, Eternal, and Imperishable is No-thing. The negation of the Welsh poets was not atheism, not annihilation, not a denial of being, but simply a denial of all accidental and perishable attributes or qualities. Catwg or Cadog, the Wise, is made to say :

No Living but God,
No Good but God,
No Wise but God,
No Knowing but God,
No Power but God,
No Love but God,
No Just but God,
No Omniscient but God,
No Strong but God,
No Endless but God,
No Judgment but God,
No Lord but God,
No Eternal but God,
No Infinite but God,
No Whole but God,
No Enough but God,
No-thing but God.

been quite sufficient to serve as a proof to the philosophers by profession that this Nirvana, which could not become an object of perception by the senses, nor of conception by the categories of the understanding, the anakhata, the ineffable, as Buddha calls it,[26] could be nothing more or less than the Nothing. Could we dare with Hegel to distinguish between a Nothing (*Nichts*) and a Not (*Nicht*) we might say that the Nirvana had, through a false dialectical process, become from a relative Nothing an absolute Not. This was the work of the theologians and of the orthodox philosophers. But a religion has never been founded by such teaching, and a man like Buddha, who knew mankind, must have known that he could not with such weapons overturn the tyranny of the Brahmans. Either we must bring ourselves to believe that Buddha taught his disciples two diametrically opposed doctrines on Nirvana, say an exoteric and esoteric one, or we must allow *that* view of Nirvana to have been the original view of the founder of this marvellous religion, which corresponds best with the simple, clear, and practical character of Buddha.

I have now said all that can be said in vindication of Buddha within the brief time allowed to these discourses. But I should be sorry if you carried away the impression that Buddhism contained nothing but empty, useless speculations; permit me, therefore, to read to you, in conclusion, a short Buddhist Parable, which will show you Buddhism in a more human form. It is borrowed from a work which will soon appear, and which contains the translation of the Parables used by the Buddhists to obtain acceptance for their doctrines amongst the people. I shall only omit some technical expressions and minor details which are of no importance.[27]

[26] *v.* 218.

[27] This parable was given at the time, September 1869, from a Burmese text, translated by H. T. Rogers, and printed in 1870, in '*Buddhaghosha's Parables*, translated from the Burmese by H. T. Rogers; with an Introduction containing Buddha's Dhammapada, or the Path of Virtue, translated from Pâli by F. Max Müller.' The Pâli text was at that time not accessible, but it has lately been published by J. H. Thiessen (*Die Legende von Kisâ Gosami*, Kiel, 1880), from a MS. in the Royal Library of Copenhagen. It forms part of Buddhagosa's commentary on the Dhammapada, and occurs twice—once in illustration of verse 114, where it is given complete, and again in illustration of verse 287. Fausböll had omitted it in his extracts from Buddhaghosa, in his edition of Dhammapada, Copenhagen, 1855.

KISA GOTAMI

A Buddhist Parable, translated from Pâli.

When Kisa Gotami had been married one year she gave birth to a son, but when he had just begun to walk, he died. The young mother, who had never seen anyone die before, sent away the men who came to burn the dead body.

'I shall ask for medicine for my boy,' she cried, and, taking the dead child in her arms, she went from house to house, asking the people, 'Do you not know any medicine for my boy ?'

Then the people answered : 'Surely, thou art mad to go about asking for medicine for a dead child.'

But she said : 'I shall surely find some one who will tell me what I can do for my boy.'

Now, there was a wise man who saw her and thought, 'It may be that the poor girl has had her first child. She does not know what death is. I ought to comfort her.' And he said to her : 'My daughter, I myself know of no medicine; but I know one who knows the right medicine for thee.'

'O father,' she said, 'who is he ?'

'The Master,' he replied. 'Go and ask him.'

'I shall go, father,' she said. And she went to the Master, and bowed down before him, and, standing by his side, she said : 'Master, do you indeed know some medicine for my son ?'

'Daughter, I do,' he replied.

'What should I get for him ?' she said.

'Get only a few mustard seeds,' he replied.

'I shall get them, Master,' she said; 'but in whose house shall I get them ?'

'In any house,' he replied, 'where neither a son, nor a daughter, nor anyone else has yet died.'

'Well, Master,' she said, and bowed before him, and took her dead child in her arms, and went to the nearest village.

Standing at the door of the first house, she cried : 'Have you, perhaps, in your house a few mustard seeds ? I want them as medicine for my boy.'

'We have,' the people answered.

'Then give them to me,' she said.

And when they had brought the mustard seeds and given them to her, she asked : 'Friends, surely no son, or daughter, or anyone else has yet died in this house ?'

They answered : 'Friend, what dost thou say ? The living are few, the dead are many.'

'Then take your mustard-seeds,' she said, and threw them down; 'they will not do as medicine for my boy.'

And walking away from the first house she went on in the same manner, asking at every door. But when she could not get the mustard seeds at any house, and evening was now drawing near, she thought : 'This is a heavy task; I know now, my boy is dead. In every village the dead are more than the living.'

While she was thinking thus, her heart, which had been breaking for love to her child, grew strong. She took the child to the forest, and left him there.

Then she went back to the Master, bowed down before him, and stood silent by his side. And the Master spake to her, saying : 'Hast thou got the few mustard seeds ?'

'No, Master,' she said : 'in every village the dead are more than the living.'

Then the Master said to her : 'Thou thoughtest that thy son alone had died, but there is the eternal law for all living beings. The King of Death, like a rushing stream, carries away all beings into the ocean of destruction, long before their wishes are fulfilled.'

Then, in order to teach the Law, the Master spoke the following verse :

'Death comes and carries off the thoughtless man,
Proud of his sons and flocks that none can number,
As floods arise and carry off by night,
A happy village bound in deepest slumber.'[28]

When he had finished this verse, Kisa Gotami had made the first step towards the truth.

And afterwards she asked the Master to admit her into the order, and the Master sent her to the nuns, and allowed her to take the vow. When she had been admitted, she received the name of Kisa Gotami, the elder lady.

[28] Dhammapada, *v.* 287.

One day she came to the door of the chapel, and having lighted a lamp, she sat down. When she saw the rows of lamps going out and reviving, she was comforted, thinking, 'Like these lamps, all living beings, too, go out and revive; but those who have reached Nibbana are seen no more.'

The Master was seated at that time in his chamber, and sending forth a radiant image of himself, he sat down before her, as if preaching, and said : 'So it is, indeed, O Gotami; like lamps, all living beings go out and revive; but those who have reached Nibbana are seen no more.'

He then said : 'One moment's life of a man who sees Nibbana is better than a hundred years of those who do not see Nibbana;' and after showing her the connection between this and what she had just seen, he pronounced the following song, by way of teaching the Law :

'If man should live one hundred years on earth,
And never see the place which knows no dying,

One day of life would better be by far,
That made him see the place which knows no dying.'[29]

At the end of the lesson, Kisa Gotami, where she was sitting, obtained saintship together with all knowledge.

This is a specimen of true Buddhism, this is the language, intelligible to the poor and the suffering, which has endeared Buddhism to the hearts of millions—not the silly metaphysical phantasmagorias of worlds of gods and worlds of Brahma, or final dissolution of the soul in Nirvana—no, the beautiful, the tender, the humanly true, which, like pure gold, lies buried in all religions, even in the sandy desert of the Buddhist canon.

[29] Dhammapada, *v.* 114.

SUKHAVATI

The Paradise of Amitabha

TRANSLATION

Adoration to the Omniscient

This is what I have heard. At one time the Blessed (Bhagavat, *i.e.* Buddha) dwelt at Sravasti,[1] in the Jeta-grove, in the garden of Anathapindaka, together with[2] a large company of Bhikshus (mendicant friars), *viz.* with thirteen hundred Bhikshus, all of them acquainted with the five kinds of knowledge,[3] elders, great disciples,[4] and Arhats,[5] such as

[1] Sravasti, capital of the Northern Kosalas, residence of King Prasenajit. It was in ruins when visited by Fa-Hian (init. V. Sæc.); not far from the modern Fizabad. *Cf.* Burnouf, *Introduction,* p. 22.

[2] Sardha, with, the Pali saddhim. Did not the frequent mention of 1,200 and a half (*i.e.* 1,250), 1,300 and a half (*i.e.* 1,350), persons accompanying Buddha arise from a misunderstanding of sardha, meaning originally 'with a half'?

[3] Abhijnanabhijnataih. The Japanese text reads abhijnatabhajnataih —*i.e.* abhijnatabhijnataih. If this were known to be the correct reading, we should translate it by 'known by known people,' *notus a viris notis—i.e.* well-known, famous. Abhijnata in the sense of known, famous, occurs in Lalita-Vistara, p. 25, and the Chinese translators adopted that meaning here. Again, if we preferred the reading abhijnanabhijnataih, this, too, would admit of an intelligible rendering—*viz.* known or distinguished by the marks or characteristics, the good qualities, that ought to belong to a Bhikshu. But the technical meaning is 'possessed of a knowledge of the five abhijnas.' It would be better in that case to write abhijnatabhijnanaih, but no MSS. seem to support that reading. The five abhijnas or abhijnanas which an Arhat ought to possess are the divine sight, the divine hearing, the knowledge of the thoughts of others, the remembrance of former existences, and magic power. See Burnouf, *Lotus*, Appendice, No. xiv. The larger text of the Sukhavati-vyuha has abhijnanabhijnaih, and afterwards abhijnatabhijnaih. The position of the participle as the uttara-pada in such compounds as abhijnanabhijnataih is common in Buddhist Sanskrit. Bendall has called my attention to the Pali abhinnata-abhinnata (Vinaya-pitaka, ed. Oldenberg, vol. i, p. 43), which favours the Chinese acceptation of the term.

[4] Mahasravaka, the great disciples; sometimes the eighty principal disciples.

[5] Arhadbhih. I have left the correct Sanskrit form, because the Japanese text gives the termination adbhih. Hogo's text has the more usual form arhantaih. The change of the old classical arhat into the Pali arahan, and then back into Sanskrit arhanta, arahanta, and at last arihanta, with the meaning of 'destroyer of the enemies'—*i.e.* the

Sariputra, the elder, Mahamaudgalyayana, Mahakasyapa, Mahakapphina, Mahakatyayana, Mahakaushthila, Revata, Suddhipanthaka, Nanda, Ananda, Rahula, Gavampati, Bharadvaja, Kalodayin, Vakkula, and Aniruddha.[6] He dwelt together with these and many other great disciples, and together with many noble-minded Bodhisattvas, such as Manjusri, the prince, the Bodhisattva Ajita, the Bodhisattva Gandhahastin, the Bodhisattva Nityodyukta, the Bodhisattva Anikshiptadhura. He dwelt together with them and many other noble-minded Bodhisattvas, and with Sakra, the Indra

passions—shows very clearly the different stages through which Sanskrit words passed in the different phases of Buddhist literature. In Tibet, in Mongolia, and in China, Arhat is translated by 'destroyer of the enemy.' See Burnouf, *Lotus*, p. 287, *Introduction*, p. 295. Arhat is the title of the Bhikshu on reaching the fourth degree of perfection. *Cf.* Sûtra of the 42 Sections, cap. 2. Clemens of Alexandria (d. 220) speaks of the *Semnoi* who worshipped a pyramid erected over the relics of a god. Is this a translation of Arhat, as Lassen ('De nom. Ind. philosoph.' in *Rhein. Museum*, vol. i, p. 187) and Burnouf (*Introduction*, p. 295) supposed, or a transliteration of Samana? Clemens also speaks of *Semnai* (Stromat., p. 539, Potter).

[6] Names of Disciples in Sanskrit, Pali, Chinese, Tibetan, and Japanese MSS. Beal, *J.R.A.S.*, 1866, p. 140:

	JAPANESE MS.	SANSKRIT.	CHINESE.	TIBETAN.	PALI.
		(Burnouf, *Lotus*, pp. 1 and 126.)	(Beal, *Catena*, p. 378.)		
1	Sariputra	Sariputra	Sariputra	Sharihi-bu	Sariputta
2	Mahamaudgal-yayana	Maudgalyayana	Maudgalyayana	Mougal-gyi-bu	Moggalana
3	Mahakasyapa	Kasyapa	Kasyapa	Hodsrungs--ch'hen-po	Kassapa
4	Mahakapphina	Kapphina	Kapphina (?)	Katyabi-bu	Kappina
5	Mahakatyayana	Katyayana	Katyâyana	Kapina	Kakkayana
6	Mahakaushthila	Kausthila	Mahakotthila	Gsus-poch'he	Kotthita
7	Revata	Revata	Revata	Nam-gru	Revata
8	Suddhipanthaka (Sudi, MS.)	(Mahapantha-ka?)	Srutavimsati-koti	Lam-p'hran-bstan	Mahapantha-ka
9	Nanda	Sunanda?	Nanda	Dgah-vo	Nanda
10	Ananda	Mahananda	Ananda	Kundgahvo	Ananda
11	Rahula	Rahula	Rahula	Sgra-gchan-hdsin	Rahula (Kumara)
12	Gavampati	Gavampati	Gavampati (Pindoda; Pindola?)	Balang-bdag	Gavampati (Pindolabha-radvaga)
13	Bharadvaga	Bharadvaja	Bharadvaja	Bharadhwaja	Bharadvaja
14	Kalodayin	Kalodayin	Kaladitya	Hch'har-byed-nagpo	Kala (tthera)
15	Vakkula	Vakkula	Vakula	Vakula	Vakkali
16	Aniruddha	Aniruddha	Aniruddha	Mahgags-pa	Anuruddha (tthera)

or King[7] of the Devas, and with Brahman Sahampati. With these and many other hundred thousands of Nayutas[8] of sons of the gods, Bhagavat dwelt at Sravasti.

Then Bhagavat addressed the honoured Sariputra and said : O Sariputra, after you have passed from here over a hundred thousand Kotis of Buddha-countries there is in the Western part a Buddha-country, a world called Sukhavati (the happy country). And there a Tathagata, called Amitayus, an Arhat, fully enlightened, dwells now, and remains, and supports himself, and teaches the Law.[9]

Now what do you think, Sariputra, for what reason is that world called Sukhavati (the happy) ? In that world Sukhavati, O Sariputra, there is neither bodily nor mental pain for living beings. The sources of happiness are innumerable there. For that reason is that world called Sukhavati (the happy).

And again, O Sariputra, that world Sukhavati is adorned with seven terraces, with seven rows of palm-trees, and with strings of bells.[10]

[7] Indra, the old Vedic god, has come to mean simply lord, and in the Chhanda Paritta (*Journal Asiatique,* 1871, p. 220) we actually find Asurinda, the Indra or Lord of the Asuras.

[8] The numbers in Buddhist Literature, if they once exceed a *Koti* of Koti—*i.e.* ten millions—become very vague, nor is their value always the same. Ayuta, *i.e.* a hundred Kotis; Niyuta, *i.e.* a hundred Ayutas; and Nayuta, *i.e.* 1 with 22 zeros, are often confounded; nor does it matter much so far as any definite idea is concerned which such numerals convey to our mind.

[9] Tishthati dhriyate yapayati dharmam cha desayati. This is evidently an idiomatic phrase, for it occurs again and again in the Nepalese text of the Sukhavativyûha (MS. 26*b*, l. 1. 2; 55*a*, 1. 2, etc.). It seems to mean, he stands there, holds himself, supports himself, and teaches the law. Burnouf translates the same phrase by, 'ils se trouvent, vivent, existent' (*Lotus,* p. 354). On yapeti in Pali, see Fausböll, Dasarathajataka, pp. 26, 28; and yapana in Sanskrit.

[10] Kinkinijala. The texts read kankanajalais *cha* and kankanijalais *cha,* and again later kankanijalunam (also lu) and kankanijalanam. Beal translates from Chinese 'seven rows of exquisite curtains,' and again 'gemmous curtains.' First of all, it seems clear that we must read *g*âla, net, web, instead of *g*ala. Secondly, kankana, bracelet, gives no sense, for what could be the meaning of nets or strings of bracelets ? I prefer to read kinkinijala, nets or strings or rows of bells. Such rows of bells served for ornamenting a garden, and it may be said of them that, if moved by the wind, they give forth certain sounds. In the commentary on Dhammapada, 30, p. 191, we meet with kinkinikajala, from which

It is enclosed on every side,[11] beautiful, brilliant with the four gems, *viz.* gold, silver, beryl, and crystal.[12] With such arrays of excellences peculiar to a Buddha-country is that Buddha-country adorned.

likewise the music proceeds; see Childers, *s.v.* jala. In the MSS. of the Nepalese Sukhavativyuha (*R.A.S.*), p. 39*a*, l. 4, I likewise find svarna-ratna-kinkinijalani, which settles the matter, and shows how little confidence we can place in the Japanese texts.

[11] Anuparikshipta, inclosed; see parikkhepo in Childers' Dict.

[12] The four and seven precious things in Pali are (according to Childers) :

1.	suva*n*nam,	gold.
2.	ra*g*ata*m*,	silver.
3.	muttâ,	pearls.
4.	ma*n*i,	gems (as sapphire, ruby).
5.	ve*l*uriya*m*,	cat's eye.
6.	va*g*ira*m*,	diamond.
7.	pavâ*l*am,	coral.

Here Childers translates cat's eye; but *s.v.* ve*l*uriyam, he says, a precious stone, perhaps, lapis luzuli.

In Sanskrit (Burnouf, *Lotus*, p. 320) :

1.	suvar*n*a,	gold.
2.	rûpya,	silver.
3.	vai*d*ûrya,	lapis lazuli.
4.	sphatika,	crystal.
5.	lóhitamukti,	red pearls.
6.	asmagarbha,	diamond.
7.	musâragalva,	coral.

Julien (*Pèlerins Buddhistes*, vol. ii, p. 482) gives the following list :

1.	spha*t*ika,	rock crystal.
2.	vaidûrya,	lapis lazuli.
3.	asmagarbha,	cornaline.
4	musâragalva,	amber.
5.	padmarâga,	ruby.

Vai*d*urya (or Vaidûrya) is mentioned in the Tathagatagunajnanachintyavishayavataranirdesa (Wassilief, p. 161) as a precious stone which, if placed on green cloth, looks green, if placed on red cloth, red. The fact that vaidûrya is often compared with the colour of the eyes of a cat would seem to point to the cat's eye (see Borooah's *Engl. Sanskrit Dictionary*, vol. ii, preface, p. ix), certainly not to lapis lazuli. Cat's eye is a kind of chalcedony. I see, however, that vaidurya has been recognised as the original of the Greek *berullos*, a very ingenious conjecture, either of Weber's or of Pott's, considering that lingual *d* has a sound akin to r, and ry may be changed to ly and ll (Weber, *Omina*, p. 326). The Persian billaur or ballur, which Skeat gives as the etymon of *berullos*, is of Arabic origin, means crystal, and could hardly have found its way into Greek at so early a time.

And again, O Sariputra, in that world Sukhavati there are lotus lakes, adorned with the seven gems, *viz.* gold, silver, beryl, crystal, red pearls, diamonds, and corals as the seventh. They are full of water which possesses the eight good qualities,[13] their waters rise as high as the fords and bathing-places, so that even crows[14] may drink there; they are full of golden sand, and of vast extent. And in these lotus lakes there are all around on the four sides four stairs, beautiful and brilliant with the four gems, *viz.* gold, silver, beryl, crystal. And on every side of these lotus lakes gem trees are growing, beautiful and brilliant with the seven gems, *viz.* gold, silver, beryl, crystal, red pearls, diamonds, and corals as the seventh. And in those lotus lakes lotus flowers are growing, blue, blue-coloured, of blue splendour, blue to behold; yellow, yellow-coloured, of yellow splendour, yellow to behold; red, red-coloured, of red splendour, red to

[13] The eight good qualities of water are limpidity and purity, refreshing coolness, sweetness, softness, fertilising qualities, calmness, power of preventing famine, productiveness. See Beal, *Catena*, p. 379.

[14] Kâkâpeya. One text reads Kâkapeya, the other Kâkâpeya. It is difficult to choose. The more usual word is kâkapeya, which is explained by Panini, ii, 1, 33. It is uncertain, however, whether kâkapeya is meant as a laudatory or as a depreciatory term. Boehtlingk takes it in the latter sense, and translates nadi kâkapeya, by a shallow river that could be drunk up by a crow. Taranatha takes it in the former sense, and translates nadi kâkapeyâ, as a river so full of water that a crow can drink it without bending its neck (kâkair anatakandharaih piyate; purnodakatvena prasasye kâkaih peye nadyâdau). In our passage kâkapeya must be a term of praise, and we therefore could only render it by 'ponds so full of water that crows could drink from them.' But why should so well known a word as kâkapeya have been spelt kâkâpeya, unless it was done intentionally? And if intentionally, what was it intended for? We must remember that Panini, ii, 1, 42 schol., teaches us how to form the word tirthakaka, a crow at a tirtha, which means a person in a wrong place. It would seem therefore that crows were considered out of place at a tirtha or bathing-place, either because they were birds of ill omên, or because they defiled the water. From that point of view, kâkâpeya would mean a pond not visited by crows, free from crows. Pischel has called my attention to Mahaparinibbana Sutta (*J.R.A.S.*, 1875, p. 67, p. 21), where kâkapeyâ clearly refers to a full river. Samatitthika, if this is the right reading, occurs in the same place as an epithet of a river, by the side of kakapeya, and I think it most likely that it means rising to a level with the tirthas, the fords or bathing-places. Rhys Davids informs me that the commentary explains the two words by samatittikâ ti samaharitâ, kâkapeyyâ ti yatthatatthaki tire thitena kâkena sakkâ patum ti.

behold; white, white-coloured, of white splendour, white to behold; beautiful, beautifully-coloured, of beautiful splendour, beautiful to behold, and in circumference as large as the wheel of a chariot.

And again, O Sariputra, in that Buddha-country there are heavenly musical instruments always played on and the earth is lovely and of golden colour. And in that Buddha-country a flower-rain of heavenly Mandarava blossoms pours down three times every day, and three times every night. And the beings who are born there worship before their morning meal[15] a hundred thousand Kotis of Buddhas by going to other worlds; and having showered a hundred thousand of Kotis of flowers upon each Tathagata, they return to their own world in time for the afternoon rest.[16] With such arrays of excellences peculiar to a Buddha-country is that Buddha-country adorned.

And again, O Sariputra, there are in that Buddha-country swans, curlews,[17] and peacocks. Three times every night, and three times every day, they come together and perform a concert, each uttering his own note. And from them thus uttering proceeds a sound proclaiming the five virtues, the five powers, and the seven steps leading towards the highest knowledge.[18] When the men there hear that sound, remembrance of Buddha, remembrance of the Law, remembrance of the Assembly, rises in their mind.

[15] Purobhaktena. The text is difficult to read, but it can hardly be doubtful that purobhaktena corresponds to Pali purebhattam (*i.e.* before the morning meal), opposed to pakkhabhattam, after the noonday meal (*i.e.* in the afternoon). See Childers, *s.v.* Purvabhaktika would be the first repast, as Cowell informs me.

[16] Diva. viharaya, for the noonday rest, the *siesta*. See Childers, *s.v.* vihara.

[17] Kraunkâh. Snipe, curlew. Is it meant for Kuravika, or Karavika, a fine-voiced bird (according to Kern, the Sk. karâyikâ), or for Kalavinka, Pali Kalavika? See Childers, *s.v.* opapatiko; Burnouf, *Lotus,* p. 566. I see, however, the same birds mentioned together elsewhere, as hamsakraunkamayurasukasâlikakokila, etc. On mayura see Mahav. Introd., p. xxxix; Rv. I, 191, 14.

[18] Indriyabalabodhyangasabda. These are technical terms, but their meaning is not quite clear. Spence Hardy, in his *Manual,* p. 498, enumerates the five indrayas, *viz.:* (1) sardhawa, purity (probably sraddha, faith), (2) wiraya, persevering exertion (virya), (3) sati or smirti, the ascertainment of truth (smriti), (4) samadhi, tranquillity, (5) pragnâwa, wisdom (prajna).

Now, do you think, O Sariputra, that these are beings who have entered into the nature of animals (birds, etc.) ? This is not to be thought of. The very name of hells is unknown in that Buddha-country, and likewise that of (descent into) animal natures and of the realm of Yama (the four apâyas).[19] No, these tribes of birds have been made on purpose by the Tathagata Amitayus, and they utter the sound of the Law. With such arrays of excellences, etc.

And again, O Sariputra, when those rows of palm-trees and strings of bells in that Buddha-country are moved by the wind, a sweet and enrapturing sound proceeds from them. Yes, O Sariputra, as from a heavenly musical instrument consisting of a hundred thousand Kotis of sounds, when played by Aryas, a sweat and enrapturing sound proceeds, a sweet and enrapturing sound proceeds from those rows of palm-trees and strings of bells moved by the wind. And when the men hear that sound, reflection on Buddha arises in their body, reflection on the Law, reflection on the Assembly. With such arrays of excellences, etc.

The five balayas (bala), he adds, are the same as the five indrayas.

The seven bowdyanga (bodhyanga) are according to him : (1) sihi or smirti, the ascertainment of the truth by mental application, (2) dharmmawicha, the investigation of causes, (3) wiraya, persevering exertion, (4) priti, joy, (5) passadhi, or prasrabdhi, tranquillity, (6) samadhi, tranquillity in a higher degree, including freedom from all that disturbs either body or mind, (7) upeksha, equanimity.

It will be seen from this that some of these qualities or excellences occur both as indriyas and bodhyangas, while balas are throughout identical with indriyas.

Burnouf, however, in his *Lotus*, gives a list of five balas (from the *Vocabulaire Pentaglotte*) which correspond with the five indriyas of Spence Hardy, *viz.* sraddha-bala power of faith, virya-bala, power of vigour, smriti-bala, power of memory, samadhi-bala, power of meditation, prajna-bala, power of knowledge. They precede the seven bodhyangas both in the *Lotus*, the *Vocabulaire Pentaglotte*, and the Lalita-Vistara.

To these seven bodhyangas Burnouf has assigned a special treatise (Appendice xii, p. 796). They occur both in Sanskrit and Pali.

[19] Niraya, the hells, also called Naraka. Yamaloka, the realm of Yama, the judge of the dead, is explained as the four Apayas, *i.e.* Naraka, hell, Tiryagyoni, birth as animals, Pretaloka, realm of the dead, Asuraloka, realm of evil spirits. The three terms which are here used together occur likewise in a passage translated by Burnouf, *Introduction*, p. 544.

Now what do you think, O Sariputra, for what reason is that Tathagata called Amitayus ? The length of life (ayus), O Sariputra, of that Tathagata and of those men there is immeasurable (amita). Therefore is that Tathagata called Amitayus. And ten Kalpas have passed, O Sariputra, since that Tathagata awoke to perfect knowledge.

And what do you think, O Sariputra, for what reason is that Tathagata called Amitabhas ? The splendour (abhas), O Sariputra, of that Tathagata is unimpeded over all Buddha-countries. Therefore is that Tathagata called Amitabhas.

And there is, O Sariputra, an innumerable assembly of disciples with that Tathagata, purified and venerable persons, whose number it is not easy to count. With such arrays of excellences, etc.

And again, O Sariputra, of those beings also who are born in the Buddha-country of the Tathagata Amitayus as purified Bodhisattvas, never to return again and bound by one birth only, of those Bodhisattvas also, O Sariputra, the number is not easy to count, except they are reckoned as infinite in number.[20]

Then again all beings, O Sariputra, ought to make fervent prayer for that Buddha-country. And why ? Because they come together there with such excellent men. Beings are not born in that Buddha-country of the Tathagata Amitayus as a reward and result of good works performed in this present life.[21] No, whatever son or daughter of a family shall hear the name of the blessed Amitayus, the Tathagata, and having heard it, shall keep it in mind, and with thoughts undisturbed shall keep it in mind for one,

[20] Iti, snkhyam gachhchhanti, they are called; *cf.* Childers, *s.v.* sankhya. Asankhyeya, even more than aprameyá, is the recognised term for infinity. Burnouf, *Lotus*, p. 852.

[21] Avaramatraka. This is the Pali oramattako, 'belonging merely to the present life,' and the intention of the writer seems to be to inculcate the doctrine of the Mahayana, that salvation can be obtained by mere repetitions of the name of Amitabha, in direct opposition to the original doctrine of Buddha, that as a man soweth, so he reapeth. Buddha would have taught that the kusalamula, the root or the stock of good works performed in this world (avaramatraka), will bear fruit in the next, while here 'vain repetitions' seems all that is enjoyed. The Chinese translators take a different view of this passage, and I am not myself quite certain that I have understood it rightly. But from

two, three, four, five, six or seven nights, that son or daughter of a family, when he or she comes to die, then that Amitayus, the Tathagata, surrounded by an assembly of disciples and followed by a host of Bodhisattvas, will stand before them at their hour of death, and they will depart this life with tranquil minds. After their death they will be born in the world Sukhavati, in the Buddha-country of the same Amitayus, the Tathagata. Therefore, then, O Sariputra, having perceived this cause and effect,[22] I with reverence say thus, Every son and every daughter of a family ought to make with their whole mind fervent prayer for that Buddha-country.

And now, O Sariputra, as I here at present glorify that world, thus in the East, O Sariputra, other blessed Buddhas, led by the Tathagata Akshobhya, the Tathagata Merudhvaga, the Tathagata Mahameru, the Tathagata Meruprabhasa, and the Tathagata Mangudhvaga, equal in number to the sand of the river Ganga, comprehend their own Buddha-countries in their speech, and then reveal them.[23] Accept this repetition of the Law, called the 'Favour of all Buddhas,' which magnifies their inconceivable excellences.

Thus also in the South, do other blessed Buddhas, led by the Tathagata Chandrasuryapradipa, the Tathagata Yasahprabha, the Tathagata Maharkiskandha, the Tathagata Merupradipa, the Tathagata Anantavirya, equal in number to the sand of the river Ganga, comprehend their own Buddha-countries in their speech, and then reveal them. Accept, etc.

the end of this section, where we read kulaputrena va kuladuhitra va tatra buddhakshetre chittapranidhanam kartavyam, it seems clear that the locative (buddhakshetre) forms the object of the pranidhana, the fervent prayer or longing. The Satpurushas already in the Buddhakshetra would be the innumerable men (manushyas) and Boddhisattvas mentioned before.

[22] Arthavasa, lit. the power of the thing; *cf.* Dhammapada, p. 388, *v.* 289.

[23] I am not quite certain as to the meaning of this passage, but if we enter into the bold metaphor of the text, *viz.* that the Buddhas cover the Buddha-countries with the organ of their tongue and then unrol it, what is intended can hardly be anything but that they first try to find words for the excellences of those countries, and then reveal or proclaim them. Burnouf, however (*Lotus*, p. 417), takes the expression in a literal sense, though he is shocked by its grotesqueness. On these Buddhas and their countries, see Burnouf, *Lotus*, p. 113.

Thus also in the West do other blessed Buddhas, led by the Tathagata Amitayus, the Tathagata Amitaskandha, the Tathagata Amitadhvaga, the Tathagata Mahaprabha, the Tathagata Maharatnaketu, the Tathagata Suddharasmiprabha, equal in number to the sand of the river Ganga, comprehend, etc.

Thus also in the North do other blessed Buddhas, led by the Tathagata Maharkiskandha, the Tathagata Vaisvanaranirghosha, the Tathagata Dundubhisvaranirghosha, the Tathagata Dushpradharsha, the Tathagata Adityasambhava, the Tathagata Jaleniprabha (Jvalanaprabha ?), the Tathagata Prabhakara, equal in number to the sand, etc.

Thus also in the Nadir do other blessed Buddhas, led by the Tathagata Simha, the Tathagata Yasas, the Tathagata Yasahprabhava, the Tathagata Dharma, the Tathagata Dharmadhara, the Tathagata Dharmadhvaga, equal in number to the sand, etc.

Thus also in the Zenith do other blessed Buddhas, led by the Tathagata Brahmaghosha, the Tathagata Nakshatraraja, the Tathagata Indraketudhvajaraja, the Tathagata Gandhottama, the Tathagata Gandhaprabhasa, the Tathagata Maharkiskandha, the Tathagata Ratnakusumasampushpitagatra, the Tathagata Salendraraja, the Tathagata Ratnotpalasri, the Tathagata Sarvadarsa, the Tathagata Sumerukalpa, equal in number to the sand, etc.[24]

Now what do you think, O Sariputra, for what reason is that repetition of the Law called the Favour of all Buddhas ? Every son or daughter of a family who shall hear the name of that repetition of the Law and retain in their memory the names of those blessed Buddhas, will all be favoured by the Buddhas, and will never return again, being once in possession of the transcendent true knowledge. Therefore, then, O Sariputra, believe,[25] accept, and long for me and those blessed Buddhas !

[24] It should be remarked that the Tathagatas here assigned to the ten quarters differ entirely from those assigned to them in the Lalitavistara, book xx. Not even Amitabha is mentioned there.

[25] Pratiyatha. The texts give again and again pattiyatha, evidently the Pali form, instead of pratiyata. I have left t h a, the Pali termination of the 2 p. pl. in the imperative, instead of t a, because that form was clearly intended, while p a for p r a may be an accident. Yet I have little doubt that patiyatha was in the original text. That it is

Whatever sons or daughters of a family shall make mental prayer for the Buddha-country of that blessed Amitayus, the Tathagata, or are making it now or have made it formerly, all these will never return again, being once in possession of the transcendent true knowledge. They will be born in that Buddha-country, have been born, or are being born now. Therefore, then, O Sariputra, mental prayer is to be made for that Buddha-country by faithful sons and daughters of a family.

And as I at present magnify here the inconceivable excellences of those blessed Buddhas, thus, O Sariputra, do those blessed Buddhas magnify my own inconceivable excellences.

A very difficult work has been done by Sakyamuni, the sovereign of the Sakyas. Having obtained the transcendent true knowledge in this world Saha, he taught the Law which all the world is reluctant to accept, during this corruption of the present Kalpa, during this corruption of mankind, during this corruption of belief, during this corruption of life, during this corruption of passions.

This is even for me, O Sariputra, an extremely difficult work that, having obtained the transcendent true knowledge in this world Saha, I taught the Law which all the world is reluctant to accept, during this corruption of mankind, of belief, of passion, of life, and of this present Kalpa.

Thus spoke Bhagavat joyful in his mind. And the honourable Sariputra, and the Bhikshus and Bodhisattvas, and the whole world with the gods, men, evil spirits and genii, applauded the speech of Bhagavat.[26]

This is the Mahayanasutra called Sukhavativyuha.

meant for the imperative, we see from sraddadhadhvam, etc., further on. Other traces of the influence of Pali or Prakrit on the Sanskrit of our Sutra appear in arhantaih, the various reading for arhadbhih, which I preferred; sambahula for bahula; dhriyate yapayati; purobhaktena; anyatra; sankhyam gachhchhhanti; avaramatraka; vethana instead of veshtana, in nirvethana; dharmaparyaya (*Corp. Inscript.*, plate xv), etc.

[26] The Sukhavativyuha, even in its shortest text, is called a Mahayana-sutra, nor is there any reason why a Mahayana-sutra should not be short. The meaning of Mahayana-sutra is simply a Sutra belonging to the Mahayana school, the school of the Great Boat. It was Burnouf who, in his *Introduction to the History of Buddhism,* tried very hard

to establish a distinction between the Vaipulya or developed Sûtras, and what he calls the simple Sutras. Now, the Vaipulya Sutras may all belong to the Mahayana school, but that would not prove that all the Sutras of the Mahayana school are Vaipulya or developed Sutras. The name of simple Sutra, in opposition to the Vaipulya or developed Sutras, is not recognised by the Buddhists themselves; it is really an invention of Burnouf's. No doubt there is a great difference between a Vaipulya Sutra, such as the Lotus of the Good Law, translated by Burnouf, and the Sutras which Burnouf translated from the Divyavadana. But what Burnouf considers as the distinguishing mark of a Vaipulya Sutra, *viz.* the occurrence of Bodhisattvas, as followers of the Buddha Sakyamuni, would no longer seem to be tenable,* unless we classed our short Sukhavati-vyuha as a Vaipulya or developed Sutra. For this there is no authority. Our Sutra is called a Mahayana Sutra, never a Vaipulya Sûtra, and yet among the followers of Buddha, the Bodhisattvas constitute a very considerable portion.....

* La presence des Bodhisattvas ou leur absence interesse donc le fonds meme des livres ou on la remarque, et il est bien evident que ce seul point trace une ligne de demarcation profonde entre les Sutras ordinaires et les Sutras developpes.'—Burnouf, *Introduction*, p. 112.

CHAPTER V

CHRISTIANITY AND BUDDHISM

Who has not suffered lately from Theosophy and Esoteric Buddhism ? Journals are full of it, novels overflow with it, and oh ! the private and confidential letters to ask what it all really means. It is nearly as bad as the Anglo-Jewish craze and the Original Home of the Aryans. Esoteric Buddhism has no sweet odour in the nostrils of Sanskrit and Pali scholars. They try to keep aloof of it, and to avoid all controversy with its prophets and prophetesses. But it seems hard on them that they should be blamed for not speaking out, when their silence says really all that is required. Many people, no doubt, are much distressed in their minds when they are told that Christianity is but a second edition of Buddhism. Is it really true ? they ask. Why did you not tell us all this before ? Surely you must have known it, and were only afraid to tell us. Then follow other questions : Does Buddhism really count more believers than any other religion ? Is Buddhism really older than Christianity ? And does it really contain many things which are found in the Bible ?

Now, let us suppose that all this were true. Would it make Christianity less true if it were in a minority, and if the majority of human beings were on the side of Buddhism ? Would it make Christianity less true if it were young, and if Buddhism were older by five hundred years ? Would it make Christianity less true, if Buddhism contained many things which are taught in the Bible also ?

The apostles of Esoteric Buddhism may really have been doing more good than they are aware of, if they have helped to bring questions like these before a larger public, and made people see that truth does not depend on majorities, that truth does not depend on antiquity, and that truth does not cease to be truth because it is held by others beside ourselves.

It is not to be wondered at, however, if people who know their own religion only, and even that very slightly, as far as its history is concerned, and who certainly know nothing of any other religions, except that they are the work of the devil, should be surprised at a number of more or less striking similarities which have been pointed out between Christianity and Buddhism.

Some people may still remember the charming volumes of Huc and Gabet, giving an account of their travels from China to Tibet. Nothing disturbed these excellent Roman Catholic priests so much as the Buddhist ritual in Tibet. When they visited the Buddhist temples, they could almost have imagined themselves in St. Peter's at Rome. The vestments were the same, the censers were the same, the hands of the priests were folded in the same way as at Rome, the very smell of the incense reminded them of more homely smells. What could they say? They saw but one way out of it. It was the devil who had counterfeited all this for his own vile purposes.

But if this way of escape is barred, if the similarities between Buddhism and Christianity must not be explained by the wiles of the Tempter, what remains? Two ways, and two ways only, are open. Either, one of these two religions borrowed from the other, or the similarities between them must be traced back to that common foundation which underlies all religions.

If any actual borrowing or imitation took place, it would seem to follow that it could have been Christianity only that was the borrower. Buddha died 477 B.C., and at the time of King Asoka, 259–222 B.C., his religion had been recognised as the state religion of his kingdom. Asoka was the grandson of King Chandragupta or Sandrocyptos, who was the contemporary of Seleucus; and at his court at Patalibothra lived Megasthenes, the ambassador of Seleucus. These are historical facts, and the chronological priority of Buddhism cannot well be contested. It does not follow by necessity that a more recent religion must have borrowed from a more ancient one, yet it must be admitted that we know of no other instance where a more ancient borrowed from a more recent religion.

Mere ritual coincidences, such as disturbed the peace of mind of my excellent friend, the Abbé Huc, need not agitate us. Even the existence of monasteries, both for men and women, the use of rosaries for praying, the ringing of bells for calling the faithful together, the shaving of the head by priests, and the like, can hardly be considered as essential to any religion, and none of them has been proved to have been coeval with the rise of either Christianity or Buddhism. In several cases we know the independent antecedents of these customs and ecclesiastical institutions. If Buddhist friars shaved their heads and were called Mu*n*das, or shavelings, there was a reason for it. In India different castes and even different families had each their peculiar way of wearing the hair. This custom can be traced back even to Vedic times. Buddhism, which lifted its priesthood out of and above all trammels of caste, naturally forbade the wearing of hair as a distinctive feature of caste or class, and introduced in consequence the complete shaving of the hair, not mere tonsure, among its clergy. Besides, there was the example of Buddha himself, who, on renouncing his princely rank, cut off his flowing locks, and became a shaveling.

Whatever the origin of the tonsure may have been, it could never have been an imitation of the example set by the Prince of Kapilavastu cutting off his flowing locks. The Early Christians seem to have considered it a shame for any man to have long hair; but that again is very different from the tonsure. It may show great ignorance, but I must confess that I do not know the true origin of the tonsure in the history of the Christian Church.

Oswald Felix has been publishing a number of articles in American papers, which have attracted attention in England also. His object is to prove that Christianity must have taken over not only its doctrines, but many of the incidents also as related in the Gospels, from Buddhist sources. Oswald Felix is, I believe, one of the more conscientious and fair-minded students of Buddhism. He takes his authorities either from authentic texts, the canonical writings of Southern and Northern Buddhists, or from such works as Seydel's *Das Evangelium von Jesu,* and not from Madame Blavatsky's *Isis Unveiled.* When my friends asked me to answer his articles, I urged my old plea that it is useless to argue about Homer with a man who does not know Greek, and that it would be equally useless to argue about Buddha and Buddhism with antagonists, however clever, who do not know Sanskrit or Pali. But then I was reminded that Bishops have sometimes written about Moses without knowing Hebrew, and that it was confessedly my chief object in publishing a large collection of English translations of the "Sacred Books of the East" to enable those ignorant of Sanskrit, Pali, Zend, Pehlevi, Chinese, Arabic, and all the rest, to form their own opinion of the great religions of the world.

At last came urgent letters and appeals which admitted of no refusal, and here is the substance of one of my answers.

I am told that Felix Oswald has published the following statement : "According to the Lalita-Vistara, one of the sacred books of Northern Buddhism, Buddha converted his first disciples half of them formerly followers of his precursor, Rudraka, while sitting under a fig-tree. The first disciples of Christ were seceders from the followers of John the Baptist, the precursor of the world-renouncing Messiah. 'I have seen you under the fig-tree,' says Jesus, when His converts introduce Nathanael. Nathanael then at once recants his doubts. Sitting under the sacred fig-tree is one of the mystic tokens of Buddhist Messiahship."

So far Oswald Felix. Let us now examine the case more closely. That the founders of the Christian and Buddhist religions should both have had precursors, can hardly be called a very startling coincidence, particularly when we consider how different was the relation of John the Baptist to Christ from that of Rudraka to Buddha. But that the Buddhist and the Christian Messiah should both have converted their disciples under a fig-tree does sound strange, and, being without any apparent motives, would seem to require some explanation. If there was borrowing on this point between the two religions, one would naturally think of India as the original home of the story. In India it was perfectly natural that Buddha should be represented as sitting under a fig-tree. Hermits in India lived under the shelter of trees, and no tree in India gave better shelter than the Indian fig-tree. Different Buddhas were supposed to have been sitting under different trees, and were distinguished in consequence by the trees which they had chosen as their own.

The fig-tree in Palestine, however, has nothing in common with the fig-tree in India, nor do we ever hear of Jewish Rabbis sitting under trees while teaching.

But is there a child in a Sunday-school that could not at once tell Oswald Felix and his predecessor, Dr. Seydel, that Christ never sat under a fig-tree ? We read : "Before that Philip called thee, when thou wert under the fig-tree, I saw thee." Of Christ himself sitting and teaching under a fig-tree there is no trace anywhere.

judge, I suppose, would hesitate to say after this, "There is no case." But Dr. Seydel, who seems to be Oswald Felix's chief authority, is not discouraged. He tells us that Abubekr recognised Mohammed as sent by God, because he sat under a tree, and because no one could sit under that tree *after Jesus*. This, he maintains, proves that Jesus also sat under a tree, and that this was a sign of His Messiahship. But, unfortunately, the tree thus mentioned in a Mohammedan legend is not a fig-tree, but, as we are told distinctly, a Sizyphus tree. Nor is it said that Mohammed was recognised as sent by God because he sat under a tree, under which no one could sit after Jesus had sat under it. The words are simply: "The prophet sat under the shadow of a tree, where he and Abubekr had before been sitting together. Abubekr then went to a hermit, and asked him for the true religion. The hermit asked: 'Who is the man under the shadow of the tree?' He answered: 'Mohammed, the son of Abd Allah.' The hermit said: 'By Allah, this is a prophet; no one but Mohammad, the messanger of God, sits after Jesus under that tree.' " Nowhere is it said that the hermit recognised Mohammed because he sat under a tree. Sitting under a tree never was a sign of prophethood with the Mohammedans. It simply means that he recognised him while sitting in the shadow of a tree, as the prophet who should come after Jesus.

It is not every case that breaks down so completely under the first critical examination. Still our case shows how eager certain writers are to discover Buddhist influences in Christianity, and how carefully every statement has to be tested before it can be accepted as trustworthy.

There are some similarities between Christianity and Buddhism which are much more difficult to explain. I do not mean such outward similarities as that a star stood over the palace in which the young prince who afterwards became the Buddha, *i.e.*, the Awakened or the Enlightened, was born. We know that no auspicious event could happen in India without an auspicious star. At the birth of former Buddhas also the rising of certain stars is recorded. In fact, the record of these constellations does not mean much more than if we were to say that each Buddha was born under a fortunate star.

The same applies to the miraculous conception of Baddha. The greatest miracle of all, the conception and birth of a human being, was not considered sufficiently miraculous for a Buddha. Though in the early records his birth is natural enough, in the later writings he is represented as entering the right side of his mother in the shape of an elephant.

That Buddha should have been tempted by Mara before he began the preaching of the new law is again an element that is found in the history of many religions, and does not necessitate by any means the admission of a loan either on the Buddhist or on the Christian side.

No doubt the visit paid by the old saint. Asita, to the palace, in order to worship the child that had just been born, and to prophesy his greatness, is startlingly like the visit of Simeon to the Temple, to greet the child Jesus and to prophesy the consolation of Israel. And yet the two are not alike. The hope for the coming of a Deliverer, or a Messiah, was a historical fact among the Jews, but it cannot be proved to have existed in India before the rise of historical Buddhism. We find it, indeed, in the Buddhist Scriptures, but the Buddhist Scriptures are later than Buddha, and no trace of such an expectation has been discovered anywhere in pre-Buddhistic documents.

I must confess that I was myself startled when I came across for the first time the following lines in which the incarnation of Buddha is described: "A great light appeared, the blind received their sight, the deaf heard a noise, the dumb spake one with another, the crooked became straight, the lame walked." This sounded indeed so much like the message given to John that one wished that there might be a historical channel through which it could have travelled from East to West, or from West to East. But here again we have only to look for the antecedents on both sides, and we shall find that there is no necessity at all for such a channel. We know that the answer given to the messengers of John the Baptist was only meant to say that the Messiah had really appeared, such as Isaiah and others had prophesied. As Isaiah had prophesied that "in that day shall the deaf hear the words of the book, and the eyes of the blind shall see out of obscurity, and out of darkness," therefore John, who wished to know whether the Messiah had really appeared, was told "that the blind receive their sight, and the lame walk, the lepers are cleansed, and the deaf hear, the dead are raised up, and the poor have the Gospel preached to them."

In India, too, we can trace the same expression back to a time when there could be no idea of any intercourse between

India and Judæa. As far back as the Vedic hymns we meet with the almost idiomatic expression: "The blind sees, the lame walks." When the great works of Indra are described, we are told (Rigveda ii. 15, 7) that the lame stood, and the blind saw. Again, in another place (Rigveda vii. 79, 2), we read: "Soma covers all that is naked, he heals all that is weak, nay, the blind saw, and the lame came forth."

The Buddhists therefore need not have borrowed these expressions from Hebrew or Greek, supposing that they ever understood these languages. They borrowed them where they borrowed so much of their wisdom, namely, from the Brahmans. only that they multiplied what they received tenfold and a hundredfold, till we can hardly recognise the simple stones in the gorgeous mosaic which they elaborated.

With all this I do nôt mean to deny that there are similarities between Buddhism and Christianity which are perplexing. Some of them, however, cease to perplex us, when we have traced Christianity on one side and Buddhism on the other back to their historical antecedents. Many things which seemed to be alike are then perceived to be totally different in their original intention, while others are simply due to our common human nature.

But I wonder that those who profess to be so such prelexed by certain coincidences that they feel constrained to admit a historical contact between these two religions should not feel far more perplexed by the differences that divide the two religions. If we are to suppose that Buddhism had reached Alexandria, and had filtered into Judæa, and had influenced the thoughts of the Essenes and other sects before the rise of Christianity, how are we to account for the diametrical opposition which exists between the fundamental doctrines of the two religions?

From a Christian point of view, Buddhism is atheistic. It recognises no gods in the Greek sense, no God in the Christian sense of the word. If we translated Buddhism into Christianity, it would be, to put it briefly, a belief in the Second Person, and a complete denial of the First. While Christianity is founded on a belief in revelation, such a belief would be entirely incongruous in Buddha's teaching. Buddha lived a long life and died a natural death, and nothing can be more different than Buddha's conception of Nirvana from the words uttered on the Cross, "To-day shalt thou be with Me in Paradise."

It is in comparative theology as it is in comparative philology. Before we compare two religions or two languages, we must study each of them by itself, and trace each of them as far back as we can to its first beginnings. Many words which at first sight seemed so much alike that it sounded almost foolish to doubt their identity have, after a time, been recognised as entirely unrelated. *Care* has nothing to do with *cura; heart* cannot be derived from Sanskrit *harid;* even deus has, for the time being, been divorced from the Greek *theos.* On the other hand, words which have hardly one letter in common have been traced back, in obedience to strict phonetic laws, to a common source. According to the newest lights, the Greek *parthenos* has been identified with Latin *virgo;* the Greek *prapides,* diaphragm, with German *Zwerch-fell,* nay, even *flea* with *locust.* This should be a lesson to all who are interested in a comparative study of religions. Many things are alike, and yet different in origin; many things seem unlike, and yet spring from a common source.*

*This and the previous four chapters are drawn from the writings of Professor Max Muller.

CHAPTER VI

BUDDHISM AND JAINISM

By Monier Williams

In my previous writings I have traced the progress of Indian religious thought through the various stages of Vedism, Brahmanism, Vaishnavism, Saivism, and Saktism, and have pointed out that all these systems more or less run into, and in a manner overlap, one another. We have seen that among the primitive Aryans the air, the fire, and the sun, were believed to contain within themselves mysterious and irresistible forces, capable of effecting tremendous results either for good or evil. They were therefore personified, deified, and worshipped. Some regarded them as manifestations of one Supreme Controller of the Universe; others as separate cosmical divinities with separate powers and attributes.

If the religion of the ancient Indo-Aryans was a form of Theism, it was a Theism of a very uncertain and unsettled character. It was a religious creed based on a vague belief in the sovereignty of unseen natural forces. Such a creed might fairly be called monotheism. henotheism, polytheism, or pantheism, according to the particular standpoint from which it is regarded. But it was not, in its earliest origin, idolatry. Its simple ritual was the natural outcome of each man's earnest effort to express devotional feelings in his own way. Unhappily it did not long retain its simplicity. The Brahmans soon took advantage of the growth of religious ideas among a people naturally pious and superstitious. They gradually cumbered the simplicity of worship with elaborate ceremonial. They persuaded the people that propitiatory offerings of all kinds were needed to secure the favour of the beings they worshipped, and that such sacrifices could not be performed without the repetition of prayers by a regularly ordained and trained priesthood. But this was not all. They developed and formulated a pantheistic philosophy, based on the physiolatry of the Veda, and overlaid it with subtle metaphysical and ontological speculations. They identified the Supreme Being with all the phenomena of Nature, and maintained that the Brahmans themselves were his principal human manifestation, the sole repositories and exponents of all religious and philosophical truth, the sole mediators between earth and heaven, the sole link between men and gods. This combination of ritualism and philosophy, which together constituted what is commonly called Brahmanism, gradually superseded the simple forms of Vedic religion. In process of time, however, the extravagance of Brahmanical ceremonial, and the tyranny of priestcraft, led to repeated reactions. Efforts after simplicity of worship and freedom of thought were made by various energetic religious leaders at various periods. More than one reformer arose, who attempted to deliver the people from the bondage of a complex ceremonial, and the intolerable incubus of an arrogant secerdotalism.

It was natural that the most successful opposition to priestcraft should have originated in the caste next in rank to the Brahmans. Gautama (afterwards called "the Buddha") was a man of the military class (Kshatriya). He was the son of a petty chief who ruled over a small principality called Kapilavastu, north of the Ganges; but he was not the sole originator of the reactionary movement. He had, in all probability, been preceded by other less conspicuous social reformers, and other leaders of sceptical inquiry. Or other such leaders may have been contemporaneous with himself. We have already pointed out that the philosophy he enunciated was not in its general scope and bearing very different from that of Brahmanism. The Brahmans called their system of doctrines "Dharma,"[1] and the Buddha called his by the same name. He recognised no distinguishing term like Buddhism. His simple aim was to remove every merely sacerdotal doctrine from the national religion—to cut away every useless excrescence, and to sweep away every corrupting incrustation. His own doctrines of liberty, equality, and general benevolence towards all creatures, ensured the popularity of his teaching;

[1]If an orthodox Brahman is asked to describe his religion, he calls it Arya-dharma, that is, the system of doctrines and duties held and practised by the Aryas. He never thinks of calling it by the name of any special founder or leader. Be it noted, however, that Dharma implies more than a mere religious creed. It is a far more comprehensive term than our word "religion."

while the example he himself set of asceticism and self-mortification, secured him a large number of devoted personal adherents. For it is remarkable that just as the Founder of Christianity was Himself a Jew, and required none of His followers to give up their true Jewish creed, or Jewish usages, so the founder of Buddhism was himself a Hindu, and did not require his adherents to give up .very essential principle of ordinary Hinduism, or renounce all the religious observances of their ancestors.[2]

Yet it cannot be denied that Buddhism was very different from Brahmanism, and it is a remarkable fact that, with all his personal popularity, the atheistic philosophy of Gautama was unsuited to the masses of the people. His negations, abstractions, and theories of the non-eternity and ultimate extinction of soul, never commended themselves to the popular mind.

It seemed, indeed, probable that Buddhism was destined to become extinct with its founder. The Buddha died, like other men, and, according to his own doctrine, became absolutely extinct. Nothing remained but the relics of his burnt body, which were distributed in all directions. No successor was ready to step into his place. No living representative was competent to fill up the void caused by his death. Nothing seemed more unlikely than that the mere recollection of his teaching and example, though perpetuated by the rapid multiplication of shrines, symbols, and images of his person,[3] should have power to secure the continuance

[2]In many images of the Buddha he is represented with the sacred thread over the left shoulder and under the right arm, according to orthodox Brahmanical usage.

[3]Since the Buddha became absolutely extinct, and since his system recognised no Supreme Soul of the Universe, there remained nothing for his followers to venerate except his memory. The mass of his converts, however, did not long rest satisfied with enshrining him in their minds. First they made pilgrimages to the Bodhi-tree, or "Tree of Knowledge," at Gaya, under which their great teacher obtained supreme wisdom. There they erected tumuli, or graves (variously called dagobas, chaityas, and stupas), over his relics, and worshipped these. Then adoration was paid to his foot-prints, and to the wheel or symbol of the Buddhist law. Finally, images of his person in different attitudes (to be described subsequently) were multiplied everewhere. Temples, at first, were unknown. There were rooms, or places of meeting, for Buddhist congregations to hear preaching; but it was not till a later period that these were used

of his system in his own native country for more than ten centuries, and to disseminate his doctrines over the greater part of Asia. What, then, was the secret of its permanence and diffusion? It really had no true permanence. Buddhism never lived on in its first form, and never spread anywhere without taking from other systems quite as much as it imparted. The tolerant spirit which was its chief distinguishing characteristic permitted its adherents to please themselves in adopting extraneous doctrines. Hence it happened that the Buddhists were always ready to acquiesce in, and even conform to, the religious practices of the countries to which they migrated, and to clothe their own simple creed in, so to speak, a many-coloured vesture of popular legends and superstitious ideas.

Even in India, where the Buddha's memory continued to be perpetuated by strong personal recollections and local associations. as well as by relics, symbols, and images, his doctrines rapidly lost their distinctive character, and ultimately, as we have already shown, merged in the Brahmanism whence they originally sprang.

Nor is there any historical evidence to prove that the Buddhists were finally driven out of India by violent means. Doubtless occasional persecutions occurred in particular places at various times, and it is well ascertained that fanatical, enthusiastic Brahmans, such as Kumarila and Sankara, occasionally instigated deeds of blood and violence. But the final disappearance of Buddhism is probably due to the fact that the two systems, instead of engaging in constant conflict, were gradually drawn towards each other by mutual sympathy and attraction; and that, originally related like father and child, they ended by consorting together in unnatural union and intercourse. The result of this union was the production of the hybrid systems of Vaishnavism and Saivism, both of which in their lineaments bear a strong family resemblance to Buddhism. The distinctive names of Buddhism were dropped,

to enshrine images and relics. A vast period of development separates the original Sangha-griha from such a temple as that erected over the eye-tooth of Buddha, at Kandy, in Ceylon, which is a crosly edifice, containing images and library, as well as the far-famed relic shrine behind thick iron bars.

but the distinctive features of the system survived. The Vaishnavas were Buddhists in their doctrines of liberty and equality, in their abstinence from injury (*a-hinsa*), in their desire for the preservation of life, in their hero-worship, deification of humanity, and fondness for images; while the Saivas were Buddhists in their love for self-mortification and austerity, as well as in their superstitious dread of the power of demoniacal agencies. What, then, became of the atheistical philosophy and agnostic materialism of the Buddhistic creed? Those doctrines were no more expelled from India than were other Buddhistic ideas. They found a home, under changed names, among various sects, but especially in a kindred system which has survived to the present day, and may be conveniently called Jainism.[4] Here, then, we are brought face to face with the special subject of our present paper: What are the peculiar characteristics of the Jaina creed?

To give an exhaustive reply to such a question will scarcely be possible until the sacred books of Buddhists and Jainas (or, as they are commonly called, Jains) have been more thoroughly investigated. All that I can do at present is to give a general outline of Jaina doctrines, and to indicate the principal points in which they either agree with or differ from those of Buddhists and Brahmans.[5] Perhaps the first point to which attention may be directed is that recent investigations have tended to show that Buddhism and Jainism were not related to each other as parent and child, but rather as children of a common parent, born at different intervals, though at about the same period of time, and marked by distinct characteristics, though possessing a strong family resemblance. Both these systems, in fact, were the product of Brahmanical rationalistic thought, which was itself a child of Brahmanism. Both were forms of materialistic philosophy engendered from separate kindred germs.

[4]The expression, Jainism, corresponds to Vaishnavism and Saivism just as the term Jaina does to Vaishnava or Saiva. Of course consistency would reouire the substitution of Bauddhism and Bauddha for Buddhism and Buddhist, but I fear, the latter expressions are too firmly established to admit of alteration.

[5]There is one place in India where the growth of Vaishnavism out of Buddhism, and their near relationship, are conscicuously demonstrated. I mean Buddha-gaya, with the neighbouring Vishnu temple of the city of Gaya.

For there can be no doubt that different lines of philosophical speculation were developed by the Brahmans at a very early period. All such speculations were regarded by them as legitimate phases of their own religious system. In some localities where Brahmanism was strong and dominant, rationalism was restrained within orthodox limits. In other places it diverged into unorthodox sceptical inquiries. In others into rank heresy and schism. Buddhism and Jainism represented different schools of heretical philosophical speculation which were in all likehood nearly synchronous in their origin. That is to say, Gautama, the founder of Buddhism, and Parsvanatha, the probable founder of Jainism, may have lived about the same time in different parts of India. Nor is it unreasonable to conjecture that both these freethinkers may have followed closely on Kapila, the reputed founder of the Sankhya system and typical representative of rationalistic Brahmanism.[6] By far the most popular of the three was Gautama, commonly called the Buddha. The influence of his personal character, combined with the extraordinary persuasiveness of his teaching, was irresistible. His system spread with his followers and admirers in every direction, and threw all kindred systems into the shade. Very soon Buddhistic doctrines leavened the religions of the whole Indian peninsula, from Afghanistan to Ceylon. They found their way into every home. They became domesticated in the cottages of peasants and palaces of kings. As to Jainism, centuries elapsed before it emerged from the obscurity to which the greater popularity of Buddhism had consigned it. Nor, even when its rival was extinguished, did it ever rise above the rank of an insignificant sect. At present the total number of Jainas in all India does not exceed 400,000,[7] at least half of whom are found in the Bombay Presidency.

Yet it is not impossible that the first opposition to sacerdotalism may have been due to Jaina influences, and that Indian rationalistic speculation may have been inaugurated by early Jaina leaders. We know that the Buddhist king

[6]In the Caves of Eilora, Brahmanism, Budhism, and Jainism, many be seen in juxtaposition, proving that one period, at least, they existed together, and were mutually tolerant of each other.

[7]A nineteenth century computation.

Asoka, in his inscriptions—which are referred to the third century B.C.—mentions the Jainas under the name of Nirgrantha, as if well established and well known in his time. We know, too, what has happened in our own country. Not long ago there was a reaction from extreme Evangelical religious thought in England. But because that reactionary movement is called by the name of a particular leader, it by no means follows that he was chronologically the first to set it in action. In the same way it may possibly turn out to be a fact that the Jaina Parsvatatha, rather than the Buddha Gautama, was the first excogitator of the heretical ideas and theories common to both. It seems to me, indeed, not improbable that Jainism, which is now at length assimilating itself to Hinduism, maintained its ground more persistently in India, not only because, unlike Buddhism, it sullenly refused to fraternize with Brahmanism, and to court converts from other creeds, but because the lines of demarcation which separated it from the orthodox system were in some essential points more sharp and decided than those which separated Buddhism. It is, at any rate, a fact that the Jainas claim for their system a prior origin to that of Buddhism, and even affirm that Gautama Buddha was a pupil of their chief Jina, Mahavira. Nor will it surprise us that the legendary history of Mahavira,' who succeeded Parśvanatha, and was the first real propagator of the Jaina creed, favours the theory of such a priority. True, Mahavira is described as the son of Siddhartha, which is an epithet given to the Buddha. But he is also said to have had a pupil named Gautama, and his death is fixed by the concurrent testimony of both parties of Jainas, who follow different reckonings, at a date corresponding to about B.C. 526 or 527, the usual date assigned by modern research to the Nirvana or death of Buddha being 477 or 478.

But it must not be supposed that Parsvanatha and his successor Mahavira, are regarded by the Jainas as their first supreme Jinas. They were preceded by twenty-two other mythical leaders and patriarchs, beginning with Rishabha,*

*Their names at full are:—1. Rishabha; 2. Ajita; ; 3 Samphava 4. Abhinandana; 5. Sumati; 6. Padma-prabha; 7. Suparsva; 8. Chandra-prabha; 9. Pushpa-danta; 10. Sitala; 11. Sreyas; 12. Vasupujya; 13. Vimala; 14. Ananta; 15. Dharma; 16. Santi: 17. Kunthu:

whose fabulous lives protracted to millions of years, and whose fabulous statures, proportionally extended, were probably invented in recent times, that the Jaina system might not be outdone by that of either Brahmans or Buddhists.

It is well known that the code of Manu—which is the best exponent of Brahmanism—supposes a constant succession of religious guides through an infinite succession of cycles. These cycles are called Kalpas. Every Kalpa or Æon of time begins with a new creation, and ends with a universal dissolution of all existing things—including Brahma, Vishnu, Siva, gods, demons, men, and animals—into Brahma, or the One sole impersonal self-existent Soul of the Universe. In the interval between each creation and dissolution there are fourteen periods, presided over by fourteen successive patriarchs or progenitors of the human race called Manus, who, as their name implies, are the authors of all human wisdom, and who create a succession of Sages and Saints (Rishis and Munis), for mankind's guidance and instruction.

The Buddhists, also, have their cycles of time, presided over by twenty-four Buddhas, or 'perfectly enlightened men,' Gautama being (according to the Northern reckoning) the seventh of the series. Similarly the Jainas have their vast periods superintended by twenty-four Jinas, or 'self-conquering sages.' The notion is that alternate periods of degeneracy and amelioration succeed each other with symmetrical regularity. Each cycle embraces vast terms of years; for in the determination of the world's epochs Indian arithmeticians anticipated centuries ago the wildest hypotheses of modern European science. A single Kalpa, or Æon, of the Brahmans consists of 4,320,000,000 years. It is divided into a thousand periods of four ages (called Satya, Treta, Dvapara, and Kali), under which there is gradual degeneration until the depths of degeneracy are reached in the Kali age. The Buddhist

18. Ara; 19. Malli; 20. Suivrata; 21. Nimi; 22. Nemi; 23. Parsvanatha; 24. Mahavira, or Vardhamana. The first of these lived 8,400,000 years, and attained a stature equal to 500 bows' length. The age and stature of the second was something less. The twenty-third lived a hundred years, and was little taller than an ordinary man. The twenty-fourth lived only forty years, and was formed like a man of the present day. The Buddhist hold that their Buddha Gautama was much above the usual height.

Kalpas are similar, but the Jaina cycles have a distinctive character of their own. They proceed in pairs, one of which is called 'descending,' (*Avasarpini*), and the other 'ascending,' (*Utsarpini*). Of these the descending cycle has six stages, or periods, each comprising one hundred million years, and called 'good-good,' 'good,' 'good-bad,' 'bad-good,' 'bad,' 'bad-bad,' during which mankind gradually deteriorates; while the ascending cycle has also six similar periods called 'bad-bad,' 'bad,' 'bad-good,' 'good-bad,' 'good,' 'good-good,' during which the human race gradually improves till it reaches the culminating pinnacle of absolute perfection. In illustration we are told to imagine a vast serpent, whose body, coiled round in infinite space in an endless circle, supports and guides the movement of the earth in its eternal progress. The head and tail of the serpent meet, and the notion is that the earth's movement alternates after the manner of the oscillating motion of a balance-wheel acted on by the coiling and uncoiling of a steel spring. First the earth moves from the head towards the tail in a downward course, and then reversing the direction moves upwards from the tail to the head. At present we are supposed to be in the descending cycle. Twenty-four Jinas have already appeared in this cycle, while twenty-four were manifested in the past ascending cycle, and twenty-four will be manifested in the future.

In Brahmanism, Buddhism, and Jainism, the idea seems to be that the tendency to deterioration would very soon land mankind in a condition of hopeless degeneracy unless counteracted by the remedial influences of great teachers, prophets, and deliverers. In the legendary history of the Buddha Gautama, he is described in terms which almost assimilate his character to the Christian conception of a Redeemer: he is even reported to have said—"Let all the evils (or sins) flowing from the corruption of the fourth or degenerate age (called *Kali*) fall upon me, but let the world be redeemed."

And what are the precise character and functions of a Jina? This inquiry must, of course, form an important part of our present subject, and the reply is really involved in the answer to another question: What is the great end and object of Jainism? Briefly, it may be stated that Jainism, like Brahmanism and Buddhism, aims at getting rid of the burden of repeated existences. Three root-ideas may be said to lie at the foundation of all three systems:—first, that personal existence is protracted through an innumerable succession of bodies by the almighty power of man's own acts; secondly, that mundane life is an evil, and that man finds his perfection in the cessation of all acts, and the consequent extinction of all personal existence; thirdly, that such perfection is alone attained through self-mortification, abstract meditation, and true knowledge. In these crucial doctrines, the theory of Brahmanism is superior to that of Buddhism and Jainism. According to the Brahmans, the living soul of man has an eternal existence both retrospectively and prospectively, and only exists separately from the One Supreme Eternal Soul because that Supreme Soul wills the temporary separate personality of countless individual spirits, dissevering them from his own essence and causing them to pass through a succession of bodies, till, after a long course of discipline, they are permitted to blend once more with their great Eternal Source. With the Brahmans existence in the abstract is not an evil. It is only an evil when it involves the continued separation of the personal soul from the impersonal Eternal Soul of the Universe.

Very different is the doctrine of Buddhists and Jains. With them there is no Supreme Being, no Supreme Divine Eternal Soul, no separate human eternal soul. Nor can there be any true soul-transmigration. A Buddhist and a Jaina believe that the only eternal thing is matter. The universe consists of eternal atoms which by their own inherent creative force are perpetually developing countless forms of being in ever-recurring cycles of creation and dissolution, re-creation and re-dissolution. This is symbolized by a wheel revolving for ever in perpetual progression and retrogression.[9]

What then becomes of the doctrine of transmigration of souls, which is said to be held even more strongly by Buddhists and Jains than by Hindus? It is thus explained. Every human being is composed of certain constituents (called by Buddhists the five Skandhas). These comprehend body, soul, and mind, with all the organs of feeling and sensation. They

[9]When Buddhism merged in Vaishnavism, its symbol of a wheel (*chakra*) was adopted by the worshippers of Vishnu.

are all dissolved at death, and absolute extinction would follow, were it not for the inextinguishable, imperishable, omnipotent force of *Karman* or Act. No sooner are the constituents of one stage of existence dissolved than a new set is created by the force of acts done and character formed in the previous stage. Soul-transmigration with Buddhists is simply a concatenation of separate existences connected by the iron chain of act. A man's own acts generate a force which may be compared to those of chemistry, magnetism, or electricity—a force which periodically re-creates the whole man, and perpetuates his personal identity (notwithstanding the loss of memory) through the whole series of his separate existences, whether it obliges him to ascend or descend in the scale of being. It may safely be affirmed that Brahmans, Buddhists, and Jains all agree in repudiating the idea of vicarious suffering. All concur in rejecting the notion of a representative man—whether he be a Manu, a Rishi, a Buddha, or a Jina—suffering as a substituted victim for the rest of mankind. Every being brought into the world must suffer in his own person the consequences of his own deeds committed either in present or former states of being. It is not sufficient that he be rewarded in a temporary heaven, or punished in a temporary hell. Neither heaven nor hell has power to extinguish the accumulated efficacy of good or bad acts committed by the same person during a long succession of existences. Such accumulated acts must inevitably and irresistibly drag him down into other mundane forms, until at length their potency is destroyed by his attainment of perfect self-discipline and self-knowledge in some final culminating condition of being, terminated by complete self-annihilation.

And thus we are brought to a clear understanding of the true character of a Jina or self-conquering Saint (from the Sanskrit root *ji*, to conquer). A Jina is with the Jains very nearly what a Buddha is with the Buddhists.

He represents the perfection of humanity, the typical man, who has conquered self and attained a condition so perfect that he not only ceases to act, but is able to extinguish the power of former acts; a human being who is released from the obligation of further transmigration, and looks forward to death as the absolute extinction of personal existence. But he is also more than this. He is a being who by virtue of the perfection of his self-mortification (*tapas*) has acquired the perfection of knowledge, and therefore the right to be a supreme leader and teacher of mankind. He claims far more complete authority and infallibility than the most arrogant Roman Pontiff. He is in his own solitary person an absolutely independent and infallible guide to salvation. Hence he is commonly called a *Tirthan-kara,* or one who constitutes a Tirtha[10]—that is to say, a kind of passage or medium through which bliss may be attained—a kind of ford or bridge leading over the river of life to the elysium of final emancipation. Other names for him are *Arhat,* "venerable;" *Sarva-jna,* "omniscient;" *Bhagavat,* "lord"

A Buddha with the Buddhists is a very similar personage. He is a self-conqueror and self-mortifier (*tapasvi*), like the Jina, and is besides a supreme guide to salvation; but he has achieved his position of Buddha-hood more by the perfection of his meditation (*yoga, samadhi*) than by the completeness of his self-restraint and austerities.

Both Jainas and Buddhists—but especially Jainas—believe in the existence of gods and demons, and spiritual beings of all kinds, whom they often designate by names similar to those used by the Hindus. These may possess vast supernatural and extra-mundane powers in different degrees and kinds, which they are capable of exterting for the benefit or injury of mankind; but they are inferior in position to the Jina or Buddha. They are merely powerful beings—temporary heavens and hells.

They may be very formidable and worthy of propitiation, but they are imperfect. They are liable to pass through other stages of existence, or even to be born again in mundane forms, until they are finally extinguished by the same law of dissolution as the rest of the universe.

Very different is the condition of the perfect saint. He is in a far higher position, for he has but one step to take before plunging into the ocean of non-existence. He is on the verge of the bliss of extinction, and can guide others to it. He can

[10]The word Tirtha may mean a sacred ford or crossing-place on the bank of a river or it may mean a holy man or teacher.

never be dragged down again to earthly imperfection and sin. He alone is a worthy object of adoration. All other beings—divine and demoniacal—are to be dreaded, not worshipped. "There is no god superior to the Arhat," says the Kalpa-sutra (Stevenson, p. 10). True worship, indeed, is not possible with Jains any more than with Buddhists. They have no supreme Eternal Being, omniscient and omnipresent, ever at hand to answer prayer, ever living to be an object of meditation, devotion, and love to his creatures.

Yet a Jaina who acts up to the principles of his faith is a slave to ceaseless round of religious duties.

The late Bishop of Calcutta told me that he once asked a pious Jaina, whom he happended to meet in the act of leaving a temple after a long course of devotion, what he had been asking for in prayer, and to whom he had been praying? He replied, "I have been asking for nothing, and praying to nobody." The fact was he had been meditating on the perfections of some extinct Jina, doing homage to his memory, and using prayer as a mere mechanical act, not directed towards any higher Power capable of granting requests, but believed to have an efficacy of its own in determining the character of his subsequent forms of existence.

It may be said that the Brahmanical idea of a saint is much the same as that of Buddhists and Jainas. But with Brahmans the perfect saint is not so solitary and independent in his spiritual pre-eminence. He is one of a numerous band of similar sainted personages. He has endless names and epithets (such as Rishi, Muni, Yogi, Tapasvi, Jitendriya, Yatendriya, Sannyasi), all of which indicate that he, like the Buddha and Jina, has attained the perfection of knowledge and impassiveness, either by abstract meditation (*yoga*), or self-mortification (*tapas*), or mastery over his sensual organs (*yama*). He may also combine the functions of a true teacher and guide to salvation (*Tirtha*). He may even, like the Buddha and Jina, have acquired such powers that any of the secondary gods, including Brahma, Vishnu, and Siva, may be subject to him. Finally, he may be himself worshipped as a kind of deity. Yet radically there is an important distinction between the Brahman and the Jaina saint, for the Brahman saint makes no pretence to absolute finality and supremacy. However lofty his position, he can never be exalted above the One Supreme Being (Brahma), in whose existence his own personal existence is destined to become absorbed, and union with whose essence constitutes the object of all his hopes, and the aim of all his aspirations.

Nothing, perhaps, better illustrates the difference between Brahmanism, Buddhism, and Jainism than the daily prayer used in all three systems. That of the Brahmans is in Sanskrit (from Rig-veda iii. 62. 10), and is addressed to the Supreme Being as giver of life and illumination. It is a prayer for greater knowledge and enlightenment: thus, "Let us meditate on that excellent glory of the divine Vivfier. May He stimulate our understandings." That of the Jainas, also called by them Gayatri, is in Magadhi Parkrit, and is in five short caluses to the following effect:—"I venerate the sages who are worthy of honour (*arhat*). I venerate the saints who have achieved perfection. I venerate those who direct our religious worship. I venerate spiritual instructors. I venerate holy men (*sadhus*) in all parts of the world." This is obviously no real prayer, but a mere formula, expressive of veneration for human excellence, like that used by the Buddhists, which is perhaps the simplest of all,—"Reverence to the incomparable Buddha;" or (as in Thibet), "Reverence to the jewel in the lotus."[11]

Brahmans, Jains, and Buddhists all alike aim at the attainment of perfect knowledge; but the Brahman, by his Gayatri prayer, acknowledges his dependence on a Supreme Being as the source of all enlightenment; while the formulas of Jains and Buddhists are simply expressive of their belief in the divinity of humanity—the efficacy of human example, and the power of unassisted human effort.

It will be evident from the foregoing outline of the first principles of Jainism, that the whole system hinges on the efficacy of self-mortification (*tapas*), self-restraint (*yama*), and asceticism. Only twenty-four supreme saints and Tirthan-karas can appear in any one cycle of time, but very mortal man may be a self-restrainer (*yati*). Every one born into the world may be a striver after sancity (*sadhu*), and practiser of austerities

[11]This is by some interpreted to mean—Reverence to the creative energy inherent in the universe.

(*tapasvi*). Doubtless, at first there was no distinction between monks, ascetics, and ordinary men, just as in the earliest days of Christanity there was no division into hishops, priests, and laity. All Jainas in ancient times practised austerities, but among such ascetics an important difference arose. One party advocated an entire abandonment of clothing, in token of complete indifference to all worldy ideas and associations. The other party were in favour of wearing white garments. The former were called Dig-ambara, sky-clothed, the latter S'vetambara (or, in ancient works, S'veta-pata), white-clothed.[12] Of these the Dig-ambaras were chronologically the earliest. They were probably the first to form themselves into a regular society. The first Jina. Rishaba, as well as the last Jina, Mahavira, are said to have been Dig-ambaras, and to have gone about obsolutely naked. Their images represent two entirely nude ascetics, whereas the images of other Jinas, like the Buddhist images, are representations of a sage, generally seated in a contemplative posture, with a robe thrown gracefully over one shoulder.

It is not improbable that the S'vetambara division of the Jainas were merely a sect which separated itself from the parent stock in later times, and became in the end numerically the most important, at least in Western India. The Dig-ambaras, however, are still the most numerous faction in Southern India, and at Jaipur in the North.[13]

And, indeed, it need scarcely be pointed out that ascetics, both wholly naked and partially clothed, are as common under the Brahmanical system as among Jainas and Buddhists. The god S'iva himself is represented as a Dig-ambara, or naked ascetic, whenever he assumes the character of a Maha-yogi—that is to say, whenever he enters on a long course of austerity, with an absoultely nude body, covered only with a thick coating of dust and ashes, sitting motionless and wrapped in mediation for thousands of years, that

[12]The actual colour of an ascetic's dress is a kind of yellowish-pink, or salmon colour. Pure white is not much used by the Hindus, except as a mark of mourning, when it takes the place of black with us.

[13]There is also a very low, insignificant, and intensely atheistical sect of Jainas called Dhundhias. They are much depised by the Hindus, and even by the more orthodox Jainas.

he may teach men by his own example the power attainable through self-mortification and abstract contemplation.

It is true that absolute nudity in public is now prohibited by law, but the Dig-ambara Jainas who take their meals, like orthodox Hindus, in strict seclusion, are said to remove their clothes in the act of eating. Even in the most crowded thoroughfares the requirements of legal decency are easily satisfied. Any one who travels in India must accustom himself to the sight of plenty of unblushing, self-asserting human flesh. Thousands content themselves with the minimum of clothing represented by a narrow strip of cloth, three or four inches wide, twisted round their loins. Nor ought it to excite any feeling of prudish disgust to find poor, hard-working labourers tilling the ground with a greater area of sun-tanned skin courting the cooling action of air and wind on the burning plains of Asia than would be considered decorous in Europe. As to mendicant devotees, they may still occasionally be seen at great religious gatherings absolutely innocent of even a rag. Nevertheless, they are careful to avoid magisterial penalties. In a secluded part of the city of Patna, I came suddenly on an old female ascetic, who usually sits quite naked in a large barrel, which constitutes her only abode. When I passed her, in company with the collector and magistrate of the district, she rapidly drew a dirty sheet round her body.

In the present day both Dig-ambara and S'vetambara Jainas are divided into two classes, corresponding to clergy and laity. When the two sects increased in numbers, all, of course, could not be ascetics. Some were compelled to engage in secular pursuits, and many developed industrious and business-like habits. Hence it happened that a large number became prosperous merchants and traders.

All laymen[14] among the Jainas are called S'ravakas, "hearers or disciples," while the Yatis,[15] or "self-restraining ascetics," who constitute the only other division of both Jaina

[14]This term, as well as Upasaka, is also used to designate the Buddhist laity.

[15]From the Sanskrit root, *yam*, to restrain. The Buddhists call this monks Sramanas, from the root *Sram*, "men who work hard at austerities," or Bhikshus, "mendicant friars." Their laymen are Sravakas, like the Jaina laymen, but are also called Upasakas.

sects, are the supposed teachers (*Gurus*). Many of them, of course, never teach at all. They were formerly callel Nirgrantha, "free from worldly ties," and are often known by the general name of Sadhu, "holy men." All are celibates, and most of them are cenobites, not anchorites. Sometimes four or five hundred live together in one monastery, which they call an Upasraya,[16] "place of retirement," under a presiding abbot. They dress, like other Hindu ascetics, in yellowish-pink or salmon-coloured garments.[17] There are also female ascetics (*Sadhvini*, or, anciently, *Nirgranthi*), who may be seen occasionally in public places clothed in dresses of a similar colour. When these good women draw the ends of their robes over their heads to conceal their features, and cover the lower part of their faces with pieces of muslin to prevent animalculæ from entering their mouths, they look very like hooded Roman Catholic nuns. I saw several treading their way through the crowded streets of Ahmedabad, apparently bent, like sisters of mercy, on charitable errands.

Of course, in Jainism anything like a Brahmanical priesthood would be an impossibility. Jainas reject the whole body of the Veda, Vedic sacrifices and ritual, and hold it to be a heinous sin to kill an animal of any kind, even for religious purposes. They have, however, a Veda of their own, consisting of a series of forty-five sacred writings, collectively called Agamas. They are all in the Jaina form of the Magadhi dialect (differing from, yet related to, the Pali of the Buddhists, the Magadhi Prakrit of Vararuchi, and the Prakrit of the plays), and are classed under the different heads of Anga, Upanga, Painna (Sanskrit, *Prakirnaka*), Mula, Chheda, Anuyoga, and Nandi. Of these the eleven Angas are the most esteemed, but the whole series is equally regarded as Sruti, or divine revelation. The Magadhi text is sometimes explained by Sanskrit commentaries, and sometimes by commentaries in the Marwari dialect, very common among merchants in the West of India. Some of the best known Angas and Upangas were procured by me when I was last at

[16]Also written Apasraya.

[17]When so attired they may be called Pitambaras, or Kashayambaras. though they belong to the Svetambara, or white-clothed party.

Bombay, through the kind assistance of Dr. Buhler; but it appears doubtful whether they would repay the trouble which a complete perusal and through examination of such voluminous writings would entail. It may safely be affirmed that their teaching, like that of the Puranas, is anything but consistent or uniform, and that they deal with subjects—such as the formation of the universe, history, geography, and chronology—of which their authors are profoundly ignorant.

The Indian commentator, Madhavacharya, in his well-known summary of Hindu sects (called Sarva-darsana-sangraha) has given an interesting sketch of the Jainas from his own investigation of their sacred writings. Their philosophers are sometimes called Syad-vadins, "asserters of possibility." because their system propounds seven modes of reconciling opposite views (*sapta-bhanga-naya*) as to the possibility of anything existing or not existing. All visible objects—all the phenomena of the universe—are distributed under the two principles (*tattva*) or categories of animate (*jiva*), and inanimate (*a-jiva*). Again. all living beings comprised under the former are divided into three classes: (1) eternally perfect, as the Jina; (2) emancipated from the power of acts; (3) bound by acts and worldly associations. Or, again, nine principles are enumerated—namely, life, absence of life, merit (*punya*), demerit, passion, helps to restraint, helps to freedom from worldly attachments, bondage, emancipation. Inanimate matter is sometimes referred to a principle (*tattva*) called Pudgala, which it is easier for Jaina philosophers to talk about than to explain.

When we come to the Jaina moral code, we find ourselves transported from the mists of fanciful ideas and arbitrary speculation to a clearer atmosphere and firmer ground. The three gems which every Jaina is required to seek after with earnestness and diligence, are right intuition, right knowledge, and right conduct. The nature of the first two may be inferred from the explanations already given. Right conduct consists in the observance of five duties (*vratas*), and the avoidance of five sins implied in five prohibitions. The five duties are:—Be merciful to all living things; practise alms-giving and liberality; venerate the perfect sages while living, and worship their images after their decease; confess your sins annually, and mutually forgive each other; observe fasting. The five prohibitions are:—Kill not; lie not; steal not; commit not adultery or impurity; love not the world or worldly honour.

If equal practical importance were attached to these ten precepts, the Jaina system could not fail to conduce in a high degree to the happiness and well-being of its adherents, however perverted their religious sense may be. Unfortunately, undue stress is laid on the first duty and first prohibition, to the comparative neglect of some of the others. In former days, when Buddhism and Jainism were prevalent everywhere, "Kill not" was required to be proclaimed by sound of trumpet in every city daily.[18]

And, indeed, with all Hindus respect for life has always been regarded as a supreme obligation. Ahinsa, or avoidance of injury to others in thought, word, and deed, is declared by Manu to be the highest virtue, and its opposite the greatest crime. Not the smallest insect ought to be killed, lest the soul of some relation should be there embodied. Yet all Hindus admit that life may be taken for religious or sacrificial purposes. Not so Buddhists and Jainas. With them the sacrifice of any kind of life, even for the most sacred purpose, is a heinous crime. In fact, the belief in transmission of personal identity at death through an infinite series of animal existences is so intense that they live in perpetual dread of destroying some beloved relative or friend. The most deadly serpents or venomous scorpions may enshrine the spirits of their fathers or mothers, and are therefore left unharmed. The Jainas far outdo every other Indian sect in carrying the prohibition. "not to kill," to the most preposterous extremes. They strain water before drinking, sweep the ground with a silken brush before sitting down, never eat or drink in the dark, and often wear muslin before their mouths to prevent the risk of swallowing minute insects. They even object to eating figs, or any fruit containing seed, and would consider themselves eternally defiled by simply touching flesh-meat with their hands.

[18]Dr. Stevenson cojectures that As'oka's famous edicts were similar proclamations, embodying all the commands and prohibitions of Buddhism and Jainism, engraved on stone to secure their permanence.

One of the most curious sights in Bombay is the Pinjrapol, or hospital for diseased, crippled, and worn-out animals, established by rich Jaina merchants and benevolent Vaishnava Hindus in a street outside the Fort. The institution covers several areas of ground, and is richly endowed. Both Jainas and Vaishnavas think it a work of the highest religious merit to contribute liberally towards its support. The animals are well fed and well tended, though it certainly seemed to me, when I visited the place, that the great majority would be more mercifully provided for by the application of a loaded pistol to their heads. I found, as might have been expected, that a large proportion of space was allotted to stalls for sick and infirm oxen, some with bandaged eyes, some with crippled legs, some wrapped up in blankets and lying on straw beds. One huge, bloated, broken-down old bull in the last stage of decrepitude and disease was a pitiable object to behold. Then I noticed in other parts of the building singular speciments of emaciated buffaloes, limping horses, mangy dogs, apoplectic pigs, paralytic donkeys, fetherless vultures, melancholy monkeys, comatose tortoises, besides a strange medley of cats, rats and mice, small birds, reptiles, and even insects, in every stage of suffering and disease. In one corner a crane, with a kind of wodden leg, appeared to have spirit enough left to strut in a stately manner amongst a number of dolorous-looking ducks and depressed fowls. The most spiteful animals seemed to be tamed by their sufferings and the care they received. All were being tended, nursed, physicked, and fed, as if it were a sacred duty to prolong the existence of every living creature to the utmost possible limit. It is even said that men are paid to sleep on dirty wooden beds in different parts of the building, that the loathsome vermin with which they are infested may be supplied with their nightly meal of human blood.

Yet I observed on other occasions that both Jainas and Hindus are sometimes very cruel to animals used for domestic purposes, believing that the harshest treatment involves no sin provided it stops short of destroying life. The following story, which I have paraphrased freely, from the Jaina

Kalpa-sutra (Stevenson, p. 11) may be taken as an illustration:[19]

> "There was a certain Brahman in the city of Pushpavati whose father and mother died. In process of time both parents were born again in their own son's house, the father as a bullock, the mother as a female dog. By-and-by the S'raddha, or festive-day for the worship of deceased parents and forefathers, came round. In the morning the son set the bullock to labour hard, that a supply of rice and milk be ready for the priests invited to the festival. When they were about to begin eating, the female dog, in which was the mother's soul, seeing something poisonous fall into the milk, snatched it away with her mouth. Upon that her son, not understanding the dog's action, flew into a passion and almost broke her back with a stick. In the evening the bullock was tied up in a cowhouse, but no food given to him after his day's toil. Both animals had become conscious of their previous state of existence, and the bullock, looking at the female dog, exclaimed, 'Alas! what have we both suffered this day through the cruelty of our wicked son!'"

As to the other precepts of the Jaina moral code, it is noteworthy that the practice of confessing sins to a priestly order of men probably existed in full force among the Jainas long before its introduction into the Christian system. A pious Jaina ought to confess at least once a year, or if his conscience happens to be burdened by the weight of any recent crime—such, for example, as the accidental killing of a noxious insect—he is bound to betake himself to the confessional without delay. The stated observance of this duty is called Pratikramana, because on a particular day the penitent repairs solemnly to a priestly Yati, who hears his confession, pronounces absolution. and imposes a penance.

The penances inflicted generally consist of various kinds of fasting, but it must be observed that fasting is with Jainas a duty incumbent on all. It is a duty only second to that of not killing. Fasting (*upavasa*) is also practised by Hindus and Buddhists, and held to be a most effective means of accumulating religious merit. Orthodox Hindus fast twice a month, on the eleventh day of each fortnight, as well as on the birthday of Krishna (*Janmashtami*), and the night sacred to Siva (*Siva-ratri*). On some fast days fruits may be eaten, but no cooked food of any kind.

[19]It is doubtless intended as a Jaina satire on the worship of deceased parents and ancestors enjoined by the Brahmanical system, and commonly practised by true Hindus.

With Buddhists and Jainas the season of fasting, religious mediation, and recitation of sacred texts, far outdoes our Lenten period. The Buddhists in some parts of the world call their fasting season Wasso (corrupted from the Sanskrit *Upavasa*). That of the Jainas is called Pajjusan or Pachchusan (for Sanskrit *Paryushana*). The Svetambara Jainas fast for the fifty days preceding the fifth of the month Bhadra, the Dig-ambaras for the seventy following days. In both cases the Pajjusan corresponds generally to the rainy season or its close. Possibly the practice of fasting during that period may be intended as an expiation for the supposed guilt incurred by the unintentional destruction of damp-engendered insects.

In regard to the duty of worshipping images, this also, like the last duty, is incumbent on all. But it is worthy of remark that images were at first only used as memorials or as simple decorations, in places consecrated to pure forms of worship. Idolatry has always been a later innovation. It has never belonged to the original constitution of any religious system. One or two differences between Hindu, Buddha, and Jaina images should be noted. Hindu images (excepting that of the ascetic form of Siva) are often profusely decorated, while Buddha and Jaina idols are always left unadorned, though sometimes cut out of the finest marble, and often having a nimbus[20] round their heads. Twenty-two of the Jina images, as well as the seven Buddhas, are represented with a coarse garment thrown over the left shoulder, the other shoulder being bare. Those of the first and last Jinas (Rishabha and Mahavira) are completely nude; and Jina images, like some of those of the Buddha, are often erect. Moreover, the idols of the Buddha Gautama represent him in four principal attitudes. He is (1) seated in deep contemplation; or (2) is seated while engaged in teaching, with the tip of the forefinger of one hand applied to the fingers of the other hand; or (3) he is a mendicant ascetic in a standing posture; or (4) he is recumbent just before his decease. In the first or contemplative attitude, he is indifferent to everything except intense concentration of

[20]The idea of encircling the heads of saints with a disc of light probably existed in India long before Christianity.

thought on the problem of perfect knowledge. According to others, he is supposed to be thinking of nothing, or, if that is impossible, his thoughts are concentrated on the tip of his nose, till he does not even think of that. Or there may be a modification of this meditative attitude, in which his mind is apparently engaged in ecstatic contemplation of the short distance which still separates him from the goal of annihilation.

The first contemplative attitude is by far the commonest. The sage is seen seated (generally on a full-blown lotus) with his legs folded under him, the left palm supinate on his lap, and the right hand extended over the right leg. He has pendulous ears, curly hair, and a top-knot on the crown of his head. His garment is thrown gracefully over the left shoulder, leaving the right bare. The modification of this attitude, representing the sage in ecstatic contemplation, has both the palms resting one above the other on the lap, and occasionally holding a circular object, the meaning of which is not well ascertained. In the second or teaching attitude, the great teacher is supposed to be marking off the points of his discourse, or emphasizing them on his fingers. This attitude expresses an important peculiarity already ponted out, as distinguishing Buddhism from Jainism—namely, that it lays more stress than Jainism on the acquisition and imparting of knowledge.

I have never seen a Jina image in a teaching attitude. The recumbent attitude of Buddha is supposed to represent him in the act of dying, and attaining Nirvana. Pious Buddhists regard this supreme moment in the life of their great leader with as much reverence as Christians regard the death of Christ on the cross. Through the kindness of Sir William Gregory, I was taken to see a colossal recumbent statue of the Buddha, at least theirty feet long[21] in the celebrated temple of Kelani, not far from Colombo, in Ceylon. The image appeared to be highly venerated by numerous worshippers, who presented offerings at the shrine. On each side were colossal images of attendants and doorkeepers (*dvara-pala*), and in other

[21]Buddhists believe that the stature of the Buddha far exceeds that of ordinary men. Muslims have similar legends about the stature of Moses.

parts of the temple figures of Buddha's demon enemies, besides idols of the Hindu deities, Vishnu, Siva, and Ganesa. All around the walls of the temple were fresco representations of incidents in the life of the Buddha. A huge bell-shaped Dagoba (*Dhatu-garbha*), of massive masonry, covered with *chunam*, was in the garden, on the right side of the temple. It doubtless enshrined ashes or relics of great sanctity. But in all these Dagobas there is no passage to any interior chamber: whatever relics they contain have been bricked up for centuries, and no record is preserved of their history or nature. On the left of the temple were the residences of the high priests and monks, in a well-kept garden overshadowed by an immense Pipal tree, supposed to represent the sacred tree of knowledge.

Both Buddha and Jina images have always certain objects or symbols (*chihna*) connected with them. Those of the Buddha are generally associated with the tree of knowledge, or hooded serpent, or a wheel, or a deer.[22] The seventh Tirthan-kara of the Jainas is specially associated with the Svastika cross—an auspicious symbol common to Hinduism, Buddhism, and Jainism. Worshippers in Buddhist and Jaina temples may be seen arranging their offerings in the form of this symbol, which is shaped like a Greek cross, with the end of each of the four arms bent round in the same direction. The question as to the origin of the emblem has called forth many learned dissertations from various scholars and archæologists. For my own part, I am inclined to regard it as a mere rude representation of the four arms of Lakshmi, goddess of good fortune, the bent extremities of the arms denoting her four hands.

With regard to the adoration of relics, one or two points of difference between the systems may be pointed out. The Hindus wholly object to the Buddhist practice of preserving and worshipping the ashes, hair, or teeth of their departed saints. I remarked in the course of my travels that articles of clothing, especially wooden shoes and cloth slippers, used by holy men during life, are sometimes preserved by the Hindus in sacred shrines, and held in veneration. They

[22]There is a legend that the Buddha taught first in deer-park near Benares.

must, of course, be removed from the person before actual death has supervened; for it is well known that in the minds of Hindus an idea of impurity is always inseparable from death. Contamination is supposed to result from contact with the corpses of even their dearest relatives. The mortal frame is not held in veneration as it was by the ancient Egyptians, and as it generally is in Christian countries. Every part of a dead body ought to be got rid of as soon as possible. Hence, it is burnt very soon after death, and the ashes scattered on the surface of sacred rivers or on the sea. Nevertheless, the bodies of great ascetics are exempted from this rule. They are generally buried, not burnt; not, however, because the mere corporeal frame is held in greater veneration, but because the most eminent saints are supposed to lie undecomposed in a kind of trance, resulting from the intense ecstatic meditation (*samadhi*) to which during life they were devoted. In former days great ascetics were not unfrequently buried alive, and that, too, with their own consent. A crowed of admiring disciples was always ready to assist at the entombment, and it hight be said in excuse that the holy men really appeared to be dead. though they were merely speechless, motionless, and senseless, in a kind of meditative catalepsy.

The Jainas hold views similar to those of the Hindus in regard to the treatment of dead bodies. They never preserve the ashes of their saints in Stupas, Chaityas, or Dagobas, or worship them, as. the Buddhists do.

In connection with this subject I may remark, that what may be called "foot-worship" (*paduka-puja*), or the veneration of footprints, seems to be common to Hindus, Buddhists, and Jainas. Even during life, when a Hindu wishes to show great respect for a, person of higher rank or position than himself, he reverentially touches his feet. The idea seems to rest on a kind of *a fortiori* argument. If the feet, as the lowest members of the body, are treated with honour, how much more is homage rendered to the whole man. Children honour their parents in this manner. They never kiss the faces of either father or mother. In some families, sons prostrate themselves at their fathers' feet. The arms are crossed just above the wrist, both feet are touched, and the hands raised to the forehead.

The notion of honouring the feet as the highest possible act of homage runs through the whole Hindu system. Small shrines may often be observed in different parts of India, sometimes dedicated to holy men, sometimes to Satis, or faithful wives who have burnt themselves with their husbands. They appear to be quite empty. On closer inspection two footprints may be detected on a little raised altar made of stone. These are called Paduka, "shoes," but are really the supposed impression of the soles of the feet. In the same way, the wooden clog of the God Brahma is worshipped at a particular shrine somewhere in Central India, and we know that the footprint of both Buddha and Vishnu at Gaya, and that of Buddha at Adam's Peak, are objects of adoration to millions.

Analogous ideas and practices prevail in Roman Catholic countries. There is a wooden image of Christ on the cross in a church at Vienna, which is so venerated that, although it is a little elevated, some worshippers stand on tiptoe to kiss its feet, while others touch its feet with their fingers, and then raise their fingers to their mouths. Similarly, at Munich, in Bavaria, numbers of worshippers may be seen kissing the feet of an image of the Virgin Mary, and most travellers can testify that images of St. Peter, not to mention the living representative of St. Peter, are treated in a similar manner.

Nothing, however, comes up to the veneration of footprints among Jainas. I visited the magnificent temple erected by Hathi-Singh at Ahmedabad, as well as the underground shrine dedicated to Adinath, and another great Jaina temple at Kaira. The first consists of a large quadrangle, approached by a beautifully carved marble gateway. The principal shrine is in the centre. All around the quadrangle is a kind of cloister, in which are about thirty subordinate shrines, each containing the image of a particular Jina or Tirthankara. All the images appeared to me to be of one type, and to resemble those of the contemplative (Dhyani) Buddha. All are carved out of fine marble, generally of a light colour, and all represent the ascetic, in his sitting posture, wrapped in profound meditation, indifferent to all external phenomena—calm, serene, and imperturbable. The attendants of the temple were either very ignorant or very unwilling to impart information. No one could tell me whether all the twenty-four Jinas had a place in the shrines. One image of perfectly black marble was described to me as that of Parsvanath.

The other temples were not very remarkable, except as gooa illustrations of "foot-worship." In one shrine I saw 1880 footprints of Nemi-nath's disciples. In another, 1452 footsteps of the disciples of Rishabha. They were covered with offerings of grain and money. All the names of these holy disciples are given in the Jaina sacred works, and it may be remarked that the disciples of Jinas, however celebrated, are never represented by images. That privilege is reserved for the twenty-four supreme Jinas themselves. I noticed that many Hindu idols were placed outside the shrines.

Certainly Jainism, when regarded from the standpoint of a Christian observer, is the oldest of all religions, if, indeed, it deserves to be called a religion at all. Yet the number of temples in certain centres of Jainism far exceeds the number of churches and chapels in the most religious Christian districts. Every Jaina who lays claim to an excess of piety or zeal builds a temple of his own. It never enters into his head to repair the temples of other religious people. At Palitana, in Kathiwar, there is a whole city of Jaina temples, some new, others decaying, and others quite dilapidated. It is by no means necessary or usual that every temple should possess either priests or worshippers. I can certify that I saw fewer worshippers even in the most celebrated Jaina temples than in any of the Buddhist temples at Columbo or Kandy. Those who came contented themselves with bowing down before the idols, and placing flowers or grains of rice and corn on he footprints of the saints.

The Yatis have a kind of liturgy, partly in Sanskrit, partly in the Jaina form of Magadhi Prakrit, partly in a kind of archaic Gujarati. No real prayers are offered, but stories of the twenty-four Jainas and their disciples are recited, with singing and an accompaniment of noisy instrumental music and beating of cymbals. Religious festivals and processions are also common. I witnessed one in the town of Kaira, on the anniversay of the death of a celebrated Yati. An immense multitude of men and women paraded the streets, preceded by a very demonstrative band of musicians. In the centre was an apparently empty palanquin, borne by six men. It contained the supposed footprints of the deceased Yati in whose honour the festival was held.

A few short extracts from the Kalpa-sutra (Stevenson, p. 103) will give some idea of the rules of discipline by which the lives of the Yatis are required to be regulated, as follow:—

"Self-restraint is to be exercised by each man, individually. Self-control is the chief of all religious exercises. If a quarrel arise, mutual forgiveness is to be asked. Three daily cleansings are enjoyed, morning, mid-day, and evening. A period of rest and fasting is to be observed yearly in the four months of the rainy season. During this period, male and female ascetics should by no means partake of rice, milk, curds, fresh butter, melted butter, oil, sugar, honey, spirits, and flesh. They must never use any angry or provoking language, on pain of being expelled from the community. Ascetics must carefully avoid contact with minute insects, small seeds, small flowers, small vegetables, &c. No ascetic must do anything whatever, or go out for any purpose whatever, without first asking premission of the Superior of the Convent. The head must be shaved, or the hair constantly clipped. No ascetic must wear hair longer than that which covers a cow."

With regard to the last injunction, it may be mentioned that the ceremony of intitation (*diksha*) usually takes place at the age of twelve or thirteen, and that part of the rite once consisted in forcibly pulling out every hair of the head (*kes'a-lunchana*). In the present day ashes are applied, and a few hairs torn out by the roots before the scissors are used.

It remains to state that the Jainas of the present period are leaning more and more towards Hindu ideas and practices. They have their purificatory rites (*sanskaras*), and a modified caste system. Not unfrequently Brahman priests are invited to take part in their marriage ceremonies. Indeed, it is by no means uncommon for intermarriages to take place between lay Jainas (*s'rvakas*) and lay Vaishnavas, especially in cases when both belong to the Baniya or merchant caste.

In short, Jainism, like Buddhism, is gradually drifting into the current of Hinduism which everywhere surrounds it, and, like every other offshoot from that system, is destined in the end to be reabsorbed into its source.

CHAPTER VII

BUDDHISM. IN CEYLON

By Reginald Stephen

Buddhism is a common name for very widely differing systems. Esoteric Buddhism is, I think, on its own showing, if not absolute nonsense, yet certainly not Buddhism. I will not allude to it any further. Northern Buddhism, as far as I have read of it, is confessedly a very free development or adaptation of that nucleus which it has in common with Southern Buddhism; in its Tibetan form it appears to be much more than a development or adaptation, to have for leading characteristics elements really incompatible with the leading characteristics of the Buddhism of the ancient books. If I am not much mistaken, the Northern Buddhism is very little known to us still, because writers on it have set forth to us in fact the Buddhism of the books, without making clear the degree in which the Northern Buddhism has deserted those standards. But of all this I have no title to write.

My remarks will be directed to certain salient point in the Southern Buddhism, as it is maintained by Buddhist authorities in Ceylon. This is the Buddhism of the Sacred Books as preserved in Ceylon and as there interpreted. There is no difference between what is maintained by Buddhist authorities in Ceylon, and what is drawn by them from the books, for they profess to be bound by these, as final standards. The practical shape which the religion takes among the mass of the people is a different matter, on which also I have a little to say.

Of the Buddhism of Ceylon I have twelve years' practical knowledge, and have made some first-hand study of the Sacred Books. If I am entitled to speak of these, it is not so much because I have read a considerable part of them in the original —for I would not compare my knowledge of Pali with that of the great European scholars—as because I have discussed the books on the spot with those who have been familiar all their lives with the traditional interpretation. I am convinced that these men know these books with a throughness, familiarity, and feeling of their meaning, to which no labour of scholars in Europe can possibly attain. They are probably often wrong on points of scholarship; but as to the drift and substantial meaning of words, phrases, or passages, their interpretation is never lightly to be set aside. The tradition on which it rests is twofold: partly, it is embodied in the ancient commentaries, which emanated mainly from Buddhaghosha and his school, and, although many centuries later than the documents commented on, are still some fourteen centuries old, and for that time have been the undisputed authorities; partly—and to this I attach even more importance— it is a tradition diffused in the habitual language and ways of thinking of the Buddhist community at large. The Sinhalese language itself is a Buddhist commentary, to the details of which it is impossible to assign a definite value, but which includes matter that can be traced back to the times at least of Asoka, in the 3rd century B.C.

I think a general distinction may be drawn between this traditional school of interpretation, and that to which European scholars incline. The Sinhalese tradition, if it differs, differs almost always in the direction of a meaning more puerile, more wooden, less interesting, less Christian. When, for instance, the word occurs which the English translate by 'sin,' an English scholar will open up the wide thoughts which the word 'sin' suggests to us, while the Indian scholars will explain it as 'killing birds or other small animals, and other kinds of sin.' Or, if the word be 'danam' (giving), the Englishman will guide his readers' thought, by the word 'charity,' to the noblest Christian ideas; the Indian interpreter will explain it 'giving rice, robes and other necessaries to monks and others.'

Such words as these have higher and lower meanings, and there are cases where a higher meaning is acknowledged by the Buddhist interpreter; but on the whole the narrow and, so to compare the case, Rabbinical interpretation is the Indian one. Now the more spiritual meaning of old writings may often have become narrowed and degraded; and there are cases when that degradation can be almost proved by the evidence of such a higher meaning in similar passages in writings of similar date. In these cases the traditonal interpretation fails, and it is *so far* discredited for other cases, as a witness to the original meaning of a passage. But such cases, I fancy, are rare; and, even in those, the tradition remains a true witness to the meaning which those terms have borne for many centuries of Buddhism.

I venture to express my opinion that this consideration applies with special force to Max Muller's translation of the 'Dhammapada.' That great scholar frequently rejects the traditional interpretation in favour of an ampler and nobler meaning. He sometimes gives Sanskrit authority for his view, but on the whole I cannot but think that he often reads into the texts what his high estimate of the human spirit leads him to expect, or his love of goodness leads him to desire.

The truth may sometimes lie between what the tradition would degrade it to and what the European would exalt it to; but the difference between the two schools is a marked one; and for my part I feel bound to see in the tradition, first an unquestionable witness to what Buddhism has been for many centuries; and secondly, a probable guide to what the makers of Buddhism meant.

I venture, therefore, to claim some weight for my judgement as to the drift of the Pali writings, because I have been guided to it by the living commentary.

It does not come within my subject to calculate the number of the Buddhists are compared with the adherents of other creeds. It is now well understood that the turn given to such a computation depends entirely on the way in which the population of China is reckoned. If all the Chinese are assigned to Buddhism, Buddhism is the most numerous religion; but then Confucianism and Taoism are not reckoned as religions at all. If half the Chinese are reckoned to Buddhism, the numbers fall below those of Christianity. Our own Dr. Legge, by his estimate of the relative numbers of Buddhists in China, brings below not only Christianity, but Hinduism and Mohammedanism in number.

What I have to urge on the point is that no such numerical estimate can be of the slighest value; for this important reason, that Buddhism differs from the religions with which it is thus numerically compared—notably from Christianity and Mohammedanism, and to some degree from Hinduism—in not claiming exclusive possession of the ground. It is a parasitic religion, ready to thrive where it can, without displacing or excluding others. A Christian cannot be a Mohammedan or a Hindu, a Mohammedan cannot be a Hindu or a Christian, but a Buddhist can be a Confucianist or a Taoist, or both, and, what is more, to a great extent a Hindu or a planet-worshipper.

For instance, in China, while Legge speaks of Confucius as 'reigning supreme, the undisputed teacher of this most populous land,' and other authorities reckon all the Chinese as Buddhists, Edkins solves the difficulty by saying that all 'three religions, Buddhism, Confucianism, and Taoism, are truly national, because the mass of the people believe in them all.' While the facts about China make it no less than false to say that the Buddhist religion is the sole refuge of five hundred millions of mankind, they show the futility of any positive statement at all about its numbers.

The case in Ceylon is equally instructive. The statues of the Hindu deities are found in the precincts of the Buddhist *viharas*; on Buddhist festivals, Buddhists visit Hindu and Buddhist temples alike; when Buddhists are sick the Hindu or devil-priest meets the Buddhist monk at the door without offence.

Further, what is really most vital—what is most practically the refuge of a Ceylon Buddhist—is not anything truly Buddhistic, but the system of astrology, charms, devil-dancing and other low superstitions which clings to the lowest part of of Hinduism. It is this, not the doctrines of the Tipitaka, which a Buddhist has to abandon when he becomes a Christian; it is this, not any rule of self-sacrifice, which the flatterers of Buddhism are fostering. What I report of Ceylon is paralleled by the recent report on the religions of Korea, by Bishops Bickersteh and Williams, who say, of that nominally Buddhist country, 'Buddhism has but little influence here. Buddhist priests are not allowed inside the capital on pain of death. The Confucian philosophy remains the religion of the learned classes; the unlearned have none, unless it be excessive reverence for, or dread of, ghosts and evil spirits.'

Hence I maintain that, while it is probably not true in any sense that Buddhists outnumber Christians, it is utterly misleading to count heads in this matter at all; because, unlike the term Jew, or the term Mohammedan, the term Buddhist is not exclusive.

I come now to the historical life of Gautama and his historical character.

Buddhism, in Ceylon and in the Sacred Books, is simply a method of escape from evil which purports to have been discovered, experienced and made known, in this present age, by a man named Gautama. The truths which he is said to have made known are held to be unchangeable, but to be lost sight of in every age, until a Buddha appears, who for the benefit of that age revives the knowledge of them. Every age —in an infinite sense—has its Buddha, and all Buddhas do and say exactly the same thing; they are born in the same family, leave home at the same hour of the night, throw away their bowls in the same stream, and son on; and the Buddha of this age is Gautama.

There is not the slighest hint that the truths come by revelation from any person superior to the Buddha, or that the Buddha is in any sense God. But, if it be asked whether Buddhists believe the Buddha to be a mere man, or, on the other hand, to be the Supreme Being, the question cannot be answered in one word. For Buddhism does not possess the idea, so familiar to us, of distinct grades of being, permanently separated from one another, such as those of the brute, the man, the god. To Buddhism all life is one: he who was a god may be now a brute, and afterwards may be a man. The difference is not one of indelible character, but of state. He is in the brute state, or 'gati;' 'tiracchanagato.' If I may parallel it by a Cambridge phrase, he has 'gone out' in the state of brute, or he has gone as man, 'manussagato;' or he may be, for the time, in a divine or in an infernal *stage of being*. But of all beings, in all stages, a Buddha is the supreme: he has reached the highest stage; he will enter on no other 'gati.' He is 'tathagato,' in the true 'gati' of a Buddha. (For, let me note incidentally, I cannot doubt that the parallels to tathagato are to be found, not in any compounds of *agato,* 'come,' but in 'sugato,' which is its synonym (entered on a good 'gati'), 'duggato,' 'tiracchanagato' and the like. And as to the element 'tatha,' it means virtually 'genuine' or 'good' as the characteristic of the 'gati,' just as 'tatharupo,' 'suitable,' and perhaps 'tadi,' 'genuine or firm.')

A Buddha is therefore the supreme being, the highest of men, and so on; but such phrases do not imply anything at all like what we mean by God. The highest deties known to Buddhism are Indra and Maha-Brahma, but the Buddha attained a position superior to theirs—not in dominion, but in enlightenment—and in fact the Jatakas represent him as having passed through the stages of being Indra and of being Maha-Brahma on his way to the final birth, in which he became a Buddha.

Such is the doctrine as to the character of a Buddha. Now what is there historically known of the Gautama, who is said to have played the part of the Buddha of this age?

From the point of view of history we must distinguish two very different sources of information, only one of which I shall hereafter speak of as historical.

The one source is the Tipitaka, or threefold collection of sacred books, which forms the canon of Southern Buddhism. These I call the books of 250 B.C. The other source is the biographies of Buddha—that of *Asvaghosha,* which is attributed to the first century A.D.; that which bears the name of *Buddhaghosha,* but is only very uncertainly ascribed to him, which may belong to the fifth century A.D.; and the Lalita Vistara, or 'beautiful detailed narrative,' which is of uncertain date, between the first and sixth centuries.

These last works are the chief source of Arnold's *Light of Asia;* while the books of 250 B.C. are the source of the lives given by Rhys Davids in Hibbert Lectures, and Oldenberg in his *Buddha.*

Back to 250 B.C., in round numbers—the date of Asoka —absolute evidence exists as to the prevalence at that time of the Buddha's teaching, and of some of the sermons and traditions. This evidence is carved in the living rock or on pillars, in different parts of India, in the form of edicts of that king under the name of Devanampiyo Pipadasi. The mention in these edicts of contemporary Greek kings points their date beyond a doubt.

Now the Sinhalese chronicle, the *Mahawanso,* states that king Asoka lived at that date, that he issued such edicts, and specially mentions that besides the name of Asoka he bore that of Piyadasi. A high degree of credibility is thus established for the *Mahawanso*. Further, the *Mahawanso* states that this Asoka sent out missionaries in nine directions to promote Buddhism (one being to Ceylon), and in particular that he sent one *Majjhimo* to preach it in the Himavanta country—'Pesesi Majjhimam theram Himavantapadesakam.'

On opening a Dagaba at Sanchi, which for other reasons was believed to be nearly of Asoka's date, there was found a small relic-box, which bore the inscription, 'Relics of the saint Majjhimo, teacher of the Himavata' ('Sapurisasa Majhimasa Himavatacariyasa'), and this in the selfsame characters as those of the edicts. The accuracy of the *Mahawanso* back to that date (cir. 250 B.C.) is thus wonderfully established. Now the same *Mahawanso* states, with full circumstance, that under this Asoka the Tipitaka or Buddhist canon was finally revised; and there is not the least reason to doubt that from that time to this it has remained substantially unchanged. The historical statements therefore contained in the Tipitaka must be consdered to be those of at least as early as 250 B.C. (I omit, of course, an immense quantity of collateral evidence by which the different stages of this argument are further supported.)

It will be evident that, in comparison with whatever historical matter is embodied in the Tipitaka, the sources of information of the other class, the biographies of Asvaghosha, Buddhaghosha, and, last of all probably, the Lalita Vistara, are utterly untrustworthy, and that when anything is included in them which is conspicuous by its absence from the Tipitaka —that is, which had it been believed *must* have been inserted —such is certainly a later fabrication. Such are most of the points of the biographies which bear any resemblance to Christianity—for instance, the miraculous birth.

In this class of later biographies, the Nidana Katha, attributed to Buddhaghosha, has claims to attention which have not, at any rate yet, been established for the Northern ones.

But the student who is really in search of historical material will not pay much attention to anything except the data which are embodied in the Tipitaka. I have shown that these must be held to have been put together as early as 250 B.C. But the same Sinhalese chronicles—it is needless for this purpose to distinguish Mahavanso from Dipavanso—whose authority has been shown to be so high, go back much further than 250 B.C., and with the same circumstantiality. They give lists of the kings who preceded Asoka, and lists of the monks who were leaders of the Buddhist congregation from Gautama's time till then.

Nothing would be more unreasonable than to refuse all credit to this earlier part of the same chronicles; it is hardly possible to distrust them so far as to doubt that the Sacred Books, substantially as we have them, existed a hundred yeras earlier.

At first sight, it may be wondered that we do not believe in them *in toto*. But there are—when the matter is looked into—good reasons for thinking that they are less trustworthy before Asoka's time than after. I will venture to express my own belief, that it was to Asoka or to the Greek influence which acted upon him, that the Buddhist literature and art owed a great stimulus; and that much became definite and systematic in his time, which had been only legendary or inaccurately remembered before.

I have thought it worth while to occupy space to this extent with a proof of the veracity of the Mahavanso chronicles, and of the existence of the present Pitaka collection three centuries or more before Christ, that I may show how immeasurably superior, for historical purposes, are the data contained in the Pitakas, to the connected biographies, which belong to various dates posterior to the Christian era: how unreasonable, indeed, it is to treat the latter as history at all.

The historical Gautama must be sought in the Pitakas.

But at this point it is most important to ask, Are the data of the Pitakas historical? are they credible, or are they so mixed with fable as to be inextricable from it? The answer must be given in view of the character of Buddhist history in general. In it, substantial facts are chronicled correctly, but adorned, not overlaid, with fictitious and often absurd circumstances. In the Mahavanso, we read such things as this: that such and such a king in his tenth year dedicated such and such a shrine; 84,000 monks came flying through the air to assist on the occasion; 63,000 gallons of melted butter were first poured over the shrine, and it was then covered with flowers to the height of thirty-three leagues! Yet inscriptions, still extant, will prove beyond a doubt that that king did inaugurate that shrine in that year. A certain king, we read, was learned in medicine; he founded hospitals all over Ceylon; he cured a cobra of indigestion; and when a monk was very ill from swallowing, in drinking water, the egg of a water-snake, which snake grew to a terrible size in his inside, the king put the monk to sleep, and fished out the snake with line, hook, and bait. Yet it is not to be doubted that the king did found the hospitals. The falsehood in these stories does not seriously interfere with the truth; it falls off harmless directly the story is handled.

The incredible elements of the Pitaka life of Gautama are mostly of this nature. At the critical moments of his life earthquakes occurred, flowers were showered by celestial beings, innumerable deities came to listen to him, till the air was so full of deities you could not put a pin between them, and so on. These are harmless enough; they belong to what is little else than a conventional mode of narration; they are little more than the epithets which we used to select, without thought of truth or falsehood, from our *Gradus*, to adorn the plain substantives of our original. The separation of the history from these requires no exercise of the critical faculty, and gives no room for arbitary decisions.

We have been led to the only source of history, the Pitakas, and we know what characters to expect in them.

The resultant biography of Gautama shows nothing supernatural and nothing which in those days was strange. Many a highborn man, in middle life, 'went out,' as it was called, from the 'household life,' into the 'homeless life,' to pursue in an ascetic career the inquiry after 'deliverance;' many such thought they had found it, gathered followers, collected them in monastic orders, were looked up to as saviours, and bore among their own adherents the title of Buddhas. The Sacred Books describe to us Gautama, with his train of disciples, as constantly coming across other leaders with trains as numerous. They take it for granted that for ages past this sort of thing had been going on. Those other leaders had renounced the world in the same sense that Gautama had, or—for this phrase 'renunciation' is an

English, not a Buddhist one—had taken the step of 'going out' from the household to the homeless life which is inaccurately called by English writers 'renunciation.' We may marvel at the state of society in which such a step could be common; and no doubt it never was as common as the books represent it, for their numbers are generally exaggerated. But we must remember that it was prescribed—if I remember right, it is in the laws of Manu—prescribed as a regular part of a Brahmin's life. '

What has been magnified into the central and characteristic fact of Gautama's life by later writers is never so treated by the historical authorities.

Nor is Gautama recorded to have performed any act of conspicuous or extraordinary goodness or self-sacrifice in his historical life. He is said to have attributed to himself in former births—when he was a hare, a stag, or what not—all sorts of noble actions; but from the point of view of history stories of former births are of course only another name for fables. That Europeans, at this time of day, should treat as examples of heroism actions which a man said he had performed before he was born, is surely a curious instance of confusion of thought. *Lessons* of virtue, or at least eulogies of virtue, they may be called; but to cite them as examples or as proofs of any other moral excellence than that which is implied in the admiration of moral excellence, is evidently absurd. The absence, in the history of Gautama, of any such conspicuous examples of heroism, is explained by Oldenberg on the ground that a Buddha, in the final stage, having acquired all virtue and all merit, needs not to perform any such actions; they belong to the stages of acquirement. But this explanation supposes the Pitaka life of Gautama to be unhistorical. It is immensely more probable that the simplest explanation is the true one; viz., that the career of Gautama was as nearly as possible that of an ordinary devoted student and teacher; and that he was distinguished not by strange acts, but by a strange degree of sympathy, insight, and constructive ability.

The life of Gautama contains nothing more strange than does the life of Shakespeare. If we can imagine Shakespeare's admirers, in the present or the next century, representing

Shakespeare as wondrously born, educated with immense expense, and spending years in studying every phase of human life under miraculous conditions; his first play set on the stage by angels, witnessed by monarchs from every part of the world, and causing raptures to innumerable hosts; representing him as hunting, with armies of beaters and rifles of incredible power and value, gigantic stags in boundless parks and forests; tortured by brutal squires, and so on —we shall have imagined a parallel to the stories on which *The Light of Asia* is constructed.

Shakespeare's life was strange enough and memorable enough; so was Gautama's; but the earlier Buddhists had no more idea that its strangeness was external than we have in the case of Shakespeare.

What then did Gautama do?

Among many who were seeking, he persuaded himself—persuaded many followers then, persuaded millions since—that he had found the secret of sorrow and the way of escape; persuaded them of this, partly by the consistency of the system under which he presented in one light the mass of the facts believed in his day; partly by an extraordinary sympathy or capacity for teaching; partly by a personal sanctity which seemed to prove that he possessed a moral secret. By sanctity here I mean almost entirely two qualities, gentleness and calm. They are the ideal virtues of the Indian mind; they are the two poles of Buddhist morality, and they seem to have been seen in the highest perfection known to India in the person of Gautama.

When we turn to his teaching, the truest thing we can say of it is, that the substance of it is its least valuable part. The addition he made to existing doctrines seems to me to have been small, and to have been mainly false. The doctrine of the series of birth and death, birth and death, as an evil net in which beings were entangled, or a pathless ocean in which they were wandering, subject to disease, old age, and disappointment; the doctrine of action, as a mechanical cause, distinguishable into merit and demerit, as the electric current is into positive and negative, a cause determining the course of a being's wandering in the ocean of rebirth; the doctrine of various grades of life, infra-human, human, and superhuman, not distinguished by indelible characters, but succeeding one another in the career of the same being, who might be demon, animal, man, god, animal, and demon again in turn—these doctrines existed. The strange great moral doctrine of the evilness of taking life—this was in force. The question how to obtain deliverance from the evil and to gain the good, how to be happily born, or, still more, how to escape unhappy birth: this was the question of the day. An elaborate psychology and an elaborate metaphysical vocabulary were ready to hand. The methods of sacrifice, of austerity, of meditation or trance—of monastic life, and mendicancy—these were the methods of his day.

None of this was due to Gautama. If it were not, as I understand it is, clear from Brahmanical and Jain works that all this existed, it would still be perfectly certain that no man, even if he could invent, could have popularised any considerable part of this within the utmost time that can be allowed to have elapsed between Gautama's first preaching and the existence of all this in historical Buddhism.

But we may well believe that Gautama was the first to make out of the chaos of thought a system whose internal consistency made it appear true. He made it consistent by casting out elements which were the truest and best. The idea of a Supreme Being—of a personal soul—these, hard to reconcile with the idea of an endless series of existences, and a mechanical *Karma;* impossible to reconcile with the utter cessation of existence—had to be dropped. And the practice of sacrifices, which witnessed to the responsible character of action, and the possibility of atonement—ideas utterly irreconcilable with *Karma,* and with non-personality—this had to be fought against. Sacrifices were also inconsistent with the inviolability of life, and the latter doctrine was exaggerated in opposition to them.

Perhaps some social or political antipathies conspired to the disparagement of sacrifices, Brahmin priests, and Brahmin astrologers; though few things among the exaggerations of the early students of Buddhism have been more exaggerated than their estimate of the hostility between Gautama and the Brahmanical system.

Gautama represented, as the central truth of his discovery,

the doctrine that suffering is inseparable from existence,—this in regard to the sentient being; suffering is inseparable from existence; and, in regard to the outer world, 'that all things are unabiding.' The next great principle was, that the cause of existence is ignorance;—virtually, ignorance of the unabiding nature of things. Through ignorance of this, we cling to things; we try to enter into relations with them; we create for ourselves a personality, which really is illusory, as are the things on attachment to which it rests. By personality we become agents, and so set in motion that deadly power of *Karma* which leads to successive births, in various degrees of misery.

Other teachers had said: This life is suffering; but satisfy the gods, and you will obtain a life in their heaven which will be happy. Gautama said, 'The misery is inherent in existence. End all, and *that* is bliss.' Buddhism seeks no heaven.

Other teachers had said: This life is illusory, because there is but one true Being, from which we are mistakenly separated or temporarily isolated by the illusion of personal individuality. Return to the One Being is happiness. Gautama says: There is no being at all that is not illusory. Buddhism seeks no Absorption.

Such was Gautama's key to metaphysics.

What was his key to morals?

The Four Noble Truths, about the sheet of suffering and escape, lead up to the Eightfold Noble Way, which is the method of escape. Here our teacher is exceedingly disappointing. The eightfold way consists of Right views, Right aims, Right thinking, and so on. At first sight it reminds me of a man in my undergraduate days who was laughed at for having run along the bank 'coaching' his college boat by crying, 'Row nicely! now do row nicely!' In other places rules are given for some, not, I am pretty sure, for all of these parts of 'Right conduct'; but they are of extremely little value as principles. They are either mechanical directions, like those for Right meditation, or they are merely restatements of the former principles, as when Right views are explained as believing that all things are uneternal, and that sorrow is inherent in existence.

It is hardly too much to say that the eightfold summary is vain and empty. There are not eight things corresponding to it. What it does embody is not eightfold but onefold, and is the root and essence of all the morals of Gautama, 'Do your best.' 'Strive' was the first and the last word of the Buddha. If you must have an end, strive to attain deliverance from existence; but in any case 'strive.'

It is the most consistent, the most pitiless—shall I say the most desperate?—assertion that was ever made, that man has no help to look for, but must help himself. 'Effort,' 'exertion,' 'self-training,' these words represent Gautama's key to morals.

Utterly unimportant for practical value in comparison with the sanction and the motive of morals are the pictures of virtue and the exhortations to it. In these Gautama must have excelled; his tact and sympathy are proved by many beautiful instances; he had wonderful facility in bringing illustrations, fables, popular stories and sayings to bear, perhaps in composing brief and striking utterances in verse; and it is impossible to doubt that he urged his exhortations with the utmost grace and tenderness. Some historical personage at least there must have been. who was held to have realised the ideal teacher under the name of Gautama. Thenceforward all that successive teachers could add or repeat, in commendation of the favourite virtues of gentleness and calm, was gathered to his writings and ascribed to him.

The Buddhist records are not without some instances of real examples of virtue in historical lives; but the fatal defect of the whole literature, from this point of view, is that the immense majority of the lessons of virtue are fictitious; entirely dissociated from this life in which we really live, and connected with that series of former births by a belief in which the sense of the paramount responsibility of *this* life is destroyed.

From the good rules and good advice which Buddhism provides little could in any case be expected, when no adequate prospect is held out in the future, and no divine assistance is offered to man's weakness; but even more ruinous, in practice, is the conviction that the present life is not all-important, but a trifling unit in an immense series, incapable of resisting in any degree the consequences of the actions of past lives, and entailing consequences on a future existence which has only a very shadowy continuity with the present.

Now, in Ceylon, when a criminal is asked why he committed the crime, he will reply, 'I suppose it is from evil-doings in a former birth that this fault has happened to me;' and if then asked, "Will you not suffer for it in another birth,' he will reply, 'It will not be I that will suffer.' For the shadowiness of the continuity is a dogma of Buddhism; the succeeding being, in the next birth, is 'Na ca so, na ca anno': 'Not the same and not another'!

Before I leave the subject of morals, I must touch on another matter. The moral teaching of the Buddhist writings is on the whole good. In later Buddhist books there is a good deal that is impure; there are bad stories among the Jatakas, but on the whole the tone is good, though far from uniformly elevated. The character of the Buddha—except as related in the Lalita Vistara class of biographies, which, to enhance his renunciation, represent him, in luscious descriptions, as having been a gross voluptuary—the historical character of Gautama is unstained, except by pride. But the Vinaya Pitaka, or books of discipline, contain passages which, while they condemn what is wrong, exhibit a degeneration of the moral sense that would have seemed incredible. There is a long passage in the Parajika book which I can only describe as the most coldblooded collection of moral horrors that ever was put together. The only defence urged of it is that to be sure of preventing sin you must specify every possible form of it, lest any form of it, remaining unforbidden, should be thought lawful. The explanation is genuine, as regards the enumeration in equal detail of sins against the seventh commandment as of those against the eighth; but what a dreary unreality of moral feeling any such system reveals; what can be hoped of a moral system which must enumerate all the possible forms and conditions of theft, lest any theft should seem to have been left unforbidden?

But I am sorry to say I must deal more fully with this matter in the interests of truth.

What do I charge upon this passage? First, that it is an unnecessary enumeration of the forms and details of vice, which can only do harm to readers; unnecessary, inasmuch as many of the things specified are utterly outside the reach of any vileness, except the vileness of the imagination. Secondly, that in the grouping and proportionate blame assigned to different offences an almost inhuman want of moral sense is displayed. Thirdly, that with few exceptions each instance of wickedness specified is said to have been committed by some Buddhist monk. I know that this is a mere conventional formula; but it is not so read by Buddhists. What must be the effect on a Buddhist reader's idea of sin to read: 'At that time a certain monk committed such and such an hideous offence. They asked the Buddha whether it was allowable or not. He replied: It is a fault'?

What do I assert about the passage which contains all this? That it is a genuine part of the Sacred Books of Buddhism; is maintained by the most learned Ceylon Buddhists to be the very words of Buddha (nothing would induce me to believe that the Buddha ever saw it); and is defended, not as being recent, secondary, or secret, but only on the ground I have already mentioned; that it has been for twenty-two centuries and more on the threshold of the Sacred Books of Buddhism, and has provoked from Buddhists no remonstrance, no qualifying or apologetic commentary.

What do I infer from this? That the boasted morality of Buddhism has not deeply affected for good the moral tone of Buddhists at any time since it has been a prevalent religion, and that the monks, the custodians of it, have been less affected than others.

It is, I think, to be regretted that in the volume of the *Sacred Books of the East* which professes to contain the first part of the Vinaya Pitaka, this passage is not referred to. It is not of its omission that I complain; no printer would print it. What I complain of is, that it is not mentioned: that the omission is not stated or explained at the place where it occurs, nor explicitly stated anywhere; and that there is not a hint from first to last in the volume that any passage of this objectionable character exists. I do not for a moment suppose that the translators wished to conceal this part, or any part, of the matter which they have omitted—for they have omitted a large amount, some quite unobjectionable.

The grounds on which they have omitted in the English *Sacred Books* much which is printed in Oldenberg's Pali edition of Vinaya Pitaka may be gathered from the two prefaces, and are, I believe, these: Oldenberg, of whom and of whose work and personal courtesy to myself I would speak with the greatest respect, believes that these instances, or specifications, or examples of the application of rules, called in Pali 'Matikapadani,' are a later portion of the book, later than another portion, the Patimokkha, which is now found along with them, and which contains the general rules. I have no doubt he is right in a certain sense: the general rules must have existed before the instances. He may possibly be right—though he is far from having proved it—in the further sense, that the Patimokkha existed as a book before the larger book was compiled. This is not the opinion of Ceylon Buddhists, who believe the Patimokhka to be an excerpt from the Vinaya; but let it be so; let the Patimokkha, in which are the general rules, be the older nucleus. and the Matikapadani, or specific cases, be the later portion of the Vinaya. That admitted, how does the case stand? It is still admitted—it is admitted by Oldenberg himself—that all have stood together as the Vinaya book, have been held to be the words of Buddha, have been in the hands of every Buddhist monk who could read Pali (happily not many)—since when? for the last few centuries?—since 350 B.C. For all that time, it is admitted, they have formed part of the Sacred Books of Buddhism: Buddhism has been responsible for them for twenty-two centuries. Ought this not to be known when Buddhist morality is being judged? To omit them from a translation of the Vinaya Pitaka (without notice) is as if a person who thought certain chapters of Genesis were the older portions—old records which the author had embedded in newer matter—were to publish a translation of those older chapters only as the Sacred Book of Judaism and Christianity.

Oldenberg says they are a commentary on the Patimokkha. To say so is to use the word 'commentary' in a misleading sense. It is used by most writers on Buddhism as the equivalent to Atthakatha—the uncanonical commentary on a canonical book. But this is a part of the canonical book itself, never called a commentary till it was called so by Oldenberg. He is wrong also—in the opinion of Ceylon Buddhists—in calling the Patimokkha a canonical book. It is not (in technical language) *mul pota,* but an *at pota*—not an original book, but a *handbook,* an extract for liturgical purposes. This idea of the *at pota* is familiar to Buddhists; and an *at pota* is distinguished by well-known marks from a *mul pota.* That, however, is chiefly a matter of words; the essence of the matter is this, that the horrible portion I have referred to is, and has been from the earliest date to which external history can carry us back, a portion of the Sacred Book of Buddha.

I have now finished a very painful duty, and nothing will please me better than to find that my Buddhist friends, on second thoughts, relegate this passage to the position of an unauthorised commentary, and that Oldenberg, in the next edition, specifies more clearly the omissions that are made.

I must now turn to the comparisons between Buddhism and Christianity.

The historical treatment of the life of Gautama, as I have indicated it, which is now I believe generally received, shows nearly all the points of his biography which are relied on as parallel to belong to the unhistorical Lalita Vistara and the rest. Whether these Northern biographies borrowed from Christianity is an interesting question, which depends on the date of Asvaghosha—which some put as early as 70 B.C., some as late as 70 A.D. (of this historical question I know nothing); on the veracity of the early Christian traditions as to the travels of Apostles; and on the degree of intercourse between Kanishka's Indian court and the Western countries.

But even were all admitted, the resemblances to Christianity are small and few. When a critic like Seydel is obliged to lay stress upon the coincidence that Gautama is said to have attained knowledge under *ficus religiosa,* and that Christ saw Nathanael when he was sitting under the domestic fig-tree, it may be inferred that the supply of coincidences is scanty.

In the historical narrative there are, I think, only two points which bear any resemblance to anything in the life of Christ. The first is the visit of the old sage, who after the birth of Gautama predicted that he would be a Buddha, and rejoiced to have seen him. But when it is considered that there is nothing here of carrying the child to the temple to be presented, no reference to the mother (such as is falsely introduced into the *Light of Asia*), and that it is a common custom after a child is born in India to get a sage to see him and pronounce his horoscope—it is difficult to see more than a slightly interesting coincidence.

The other is the so-called temptation of Buddha by Mara. Now Mara is rather the opponent than the tempter. He did not try, according to the early records, to lead Gautama into sin, so much as to stop his career. And that while the celestial beings were entreating Gautama to become the Buddha or to preach his discovery, Mara should try to prevent him, was an inevitable element in the story. In its later developments Mara appears more truly as a tempter, and as temptation is one of the world-wide facts of human nature, any expression of that great truth has its value.

Other apparent instances are fictitious. This is the case with many things in the *Light of Asia*, and if that is confessedly a work of fiction, fiction must be excused. I have read somewhere that Gautama summoned his disciples with the formula 'Follow me.' As a fact, he is not represented to have said either 'follow' or 'me' but 'Come, mendicant, the doctrine has been well preached,' &c. I take up Rhys David's *Manual of Buddhism* and turn over the pages. On p. 133 I see the heading 'Parable of the Mustard Seed.' This is no parable, in the sense in which our Lord's was a parable, and it is about mustard as a drug, not as a seed, and its aim is to show the certainty of death. On the next page is the 'Parable of the Sower,' which has nothing to do with preaching or hearing, and would much more properly be called the 'Ploughman.' On p. 141 I find the 'Sabbath;' and since there is approximately a weekly festival, this is perhaps one of the least misleading of these parallels, though it is not on any particular day of the week, nor are its rules at all like those of the Jewish Sabbath. On p. 142 I come to 'Lent,' though 'Was' is not a fast, does not precede a feast, and does not last forty days, or occur in the spring. Then comes 'Ordination.' though no priestly or ministerial office is conferred,—it is really admission to the brotherhood. Other books give us deacons, priests, and the rest—all as well founded. Much more serious turns of this kind are often given in translation to moral and religious words,—much more serious, though not to be so briefly exposed. Thus by a multitude of little parodies, nearly all of them misleading, a total impression is conveyed which is very far removed from truth. Likenesses to Christianity, and most touching ones, there are; but they are generally in the expression of man's weakness and need, not in the method of meeting it.

Although this is not its place, I must not end without a word about Nirvana. It is certain that the Nirvana of the books and of present Ceylon conviction is the state in which there is not left any capacity for re-birth—anything which could give a handle to renewed existence. He who is in Nirvana neither sees. knows, wills, nor exists. To inquire whether the soul survives in Nirvana is a question that cannot be asked, since there never was a soul. It is equally impossible to say that the soul is destroyed, for the same reason. Nothing that man can conceive of remains to him who is in that state. Whether anything is to be had there which is compatible with the absence of consciousness, personality, life, and of existence, is a question which Buddha is said to have declined to settle. The whole of Buddhism, from beginning to end, denies that anything can be affirmed of Nirvana which would not be false.

And yet it is equally certain that Nirvana is habitually spoken of as happiness, and praised in positive terms.

I believe the explanation lies in this: that the crisis of Nirvana is not death, the dissolution of the last life, but the attainment of the condition in which re-birth is impossible, and a final death within reach. This might be called the potentiality of final Nirvana, and it is inaccurately imagined —for of course the whole thing is imaginaton at the best—to be happiness to have attained that potential stage, and to know that one has no more births before one. The attainment of Nirvana, thus inaccurately thought of, is possible in life; its final achievement, in the last death, is Parinirvana. My opinion is that the notion came in this way. Roughly looking at the matter, existence is misery—therefore happiness is non-existence. In experience, to be independent of outward comforts, human praise, and the like, is happiness. In further experience, to Indian sages at least, to abstract oneself from all objects of sense and memory--the state of trance —is greater happiness still. *A fortiori*—and here language leaves the guidance of experience—more complete abstraction, from consciousness even, would be better still. And so the two lines of thought seem to meet, and complete cessation of being is called the highest good. The Buddhist starts from experience and launches into the region of imagination, where he pursues the matter without seeing that he has reached absurdity.

In practice the Ceylon Buddhist, among the masses, is both better and worse than his creed. Better, because, instead of a distant Nirvana or a series of births, he has before him the next birth only, which he thinks will be in heaven if he is good, and in hell if he is bad; because he calls on God in times of distress, and has a sort of faith in the One Creator, whom his priests would teach him to deny. Worse, because his real refuge is neither Buddha nor his Books, nor his Order, but devils and devil-priests and charms, and astrology and every form of grovelling superstition. And it is that grovelling superstition that, in Ceylon at least, every word spoken in England in praise of Buddhism tends to maintain.

CHAPTER VIII

THE WHOLE DUTY OF THE BUDDHIST LAYMAN

A Sermon of Buddha

By Robert C. Childers

Much diversity of opinion appears still to exist respecting the teaching of Buddhism. According to one it is a system of barren metaphysics, according to another it is sheer mysticism; a third will tell you that it is a code of pure and beautiful morality; while a fourth looks upon it as a selfish abstraction from the world, a systematic repression of every impulse and emotion of the heart. The last view is perhaps the commonest, and one of the latest writers on Buddhism, himself a distinguished Sanskritist, quotes with approval a French scholar's impatient allusion to "the frozen world of Buddhism"—"Tout reste donc glace dans ce monde Bouddhique![1] The question is greatly complicated by the fact that many of the Buddhist authorities have confined their studies to the "northern Buddhism" of China, Tibet, and Nepal, which is something like going to Abyssinian literature to gain a knowledge of early Christianity.

It has occurred to me that in this conflict of opinion it might be of use to the general reader to lay before him a specimen of Gautama Buddha's teaching in the shape of one of his own discourses, as they have come down to us in the original Pali version of the Buddhist Bible.[2] It seems strange that this should never have been done before, since scores of popular articles on Buddhism have appeared within the last ten or twelve years; but I believe I am right in saying that this is the first sermon of Buddha that has ever been published in an English magazine.

[1]Kern. "Jahrtelling der Zuidelijke Buddhisten," p. 63. Amsterdam. 1873.

[2]Called Tripitaka, or the Three Baskets; which are Vinaya, Sutra, and Abhidharma—Monastic Discipline, Discourses, and Metaphysics. The sermon here translated is taken from the Sutra Pitaka, which consists chiefly of moral discourses.

The sermon I have selected bears in the Pali canon the name of Sigalovada, or "The Admonition of Sigala," but it is popularly known to South Buddhists by the descriptice title of Gihivinaya, or, "The Layman's Rule of Life," because it deals with the moral conduct of the Buddhist layman, as the Vinaya, or ecclesiastical code, deals with the conduct of the Buddhist monk. It was translated thirty years ago by the the famous Wesleyan missionary Gogerly, but his version is only known to the fortunate few who have access to that rare work, the "Journal of the Ceylon Branch of the Royal Asiatic Society" for 1847. My own translation is a new one, made from a collated copy of the Pali text and commentary. I have been able to correct a great number of errors in Gogerly's translation; but I have pleasure in saying that on the whole I have found it a material help, and I have not hesitated here and there to adopt a rendering of his which struck me as an unusually happy one. I have endeavoured to be strictly literal, though in a few places I have somewhat varied the wording in order to preserve the spirit of the original. I have also omitted a few unimportant repetitions of formal phrases belonging only to the framework of the sermon, and not affecting its subtsance.

I think that this remarkable discourse, delivered centuries before Christian era, speaks for itself, and requires no panegyric of mine. But I cannot forbear asking, Does it tell us of a "forzen world?" of ice-locked affections, of the healthy impulses of the heart paralyzed and withered?—nay rather, is it not full of the enthusiasm of humanity? It is no mere philosopher, it is something more than a mystic, who says to us, "Charity, courtesy, benevolence, unselfishness, are to the world what the linchpin is to the rolling chariot."

THE SERMON

Thus I have heard. On a certain day Buddha dwelt at Rajagaha in a grove called Veluvana. And the same day the young householder Sigala rose early in the morning, and went forth from Rajagaha, and standing with wet hair and streaming garments, and clasped hands uplifted, worshipped the various quarters, the east, the south, the west, the north, the nadir, and the zenith. And Buddha rose early in the morning and put on his raiment, and taking his bowl and robe went to Rajagaha to seek alms. And the Blessed One beheld the young householder, as with streaming hair and garments and clasped hands uplifted he worshipped the various quarters, and beholding he thus addressed him:

Wherefore, young man, dost thou rise betimes, and leaving Rajagaha, with wet hair and streaming garments dost worship the various quarters—the east quarter, the south, the west, and the north, the nadir and the zenith?

Master, my father when he lay on his death-ded said to me, My son, do thou worship the quarters. Honouring therefore my father's words, reverencing, revering, and holding them sacred, I rise early in the morning, and going forth from Rajagaha, with wet hair and streaming garments, and clasped hands uplifted, I worship the various quarters—the east, the south, the west, and the north, the nadir and the zenith.

Not thus, young man, should the six quarters be worshipped according to the teaching of holy sages.

How then, Master, should the six quarters be worshipped? May it please thee, Master, so to teach me thy truth that I may know how the six quarters should be worshipped according to the teaching of the holy sages.

Hear then, young man, give heed to my words and I will speak.

And the young householder Sigala answered, Even so, Lord; and thus the Buddha spoke—

Young man, inasmuch as the holy disciple has foresaken the four polluting actions, inasmuch as he is uninfluenced by four evil states to commit sin, inasmuch as he eschews the six means of dissipating wealth, therefore freed from fourteen evils, and guarding the six quarters, he walks victorious over both worlds; for him this world is blest and the next also, and on the dissolution of the body after death he is re-born in heavenly mansions.

What are the four polluting actions forsaken by him? The destruction of life is a polluting act, theft is a polluting act, impurity is a polluting act, lying is a polluting act—these four polluting actions are forsaken by him.

And what are the four evil states that tempt men to sin? Through partiality men commit sin, through anger men commit sin, through ignorance men commit sin, through fear men commit sin. But inasmuch as the holy disciple lives unifluenced by partiality, or wrath, or folly, or fear, therefore these four evil states tempt him not to sin. Whoso from partiality, wrath, folly, or fear is tempted to pervert justice, his glory shall fade like the waning moon. But whoso untempted by these refrains from perverting justice, his glory shall be made full, like the glory of the increasing moon.

And what are the six means of dissipating wealth? Strong drink, young man, and theatre-going, and evil companions, and dicing, and wandering about the streets at night, and idleness—these six bring a man to poverty.

There are six evils, young man, in being addicted to strong drink—poverty, strife, disease, loss of character, shameless exposure of the person, and impaired faculties.

Six evils attend on him who wanders about the streets at night. His life is in danger, his wife and children are uncared for, his property is unguarded, he falls under the suspicion of frequenting places of evil resort, rumours circulate concerning him, and sorrow and remorse follow in his train.

Six evils wait upon him who thirsts after wordly amusements. He is ever crying, Where is there dancing? where is there singing? where is there music? where recitation, where conjuring, where public shows?

Six evils wait upon the gambler. If he win, he begets hatred; if he lose, his heart is sorrowful. His substance is wasted, his word has no weight in a court of justice, his friends and his kinsmen despise him, and he is looked upon as ineligible for marriage—for men say, A gambler is unfit to support a wife.

Six evils attend on him who associates with bad companions. Every gambler, every libertine, every cheat, every rogue, every outlaw is his friend and companion.

Six evils attend upon the sluggard. He says it is too cold, and does not work; he says it is too hot, and does not work; he says it is too early, and does not work; he says it is too late, and does not work; he says, I am hungry, and does not work; he says, I am full, and does not work; and while he thus lives ever neglecting his duties, he both fails to acquire new property, and that which he possesses dwindles away.

Some friends are only boon companions, some are hollow friends; the true friend is the friend in need.

Sleeping after the sun has risen, adultery, revenge, malevolence, evil communications, and avarice—these six things bring a man to ruin.

He who has sinful friends and sinful companions, who is devoted to sinful practices, the same is ruined in this world and the next.

Gambling, debauchery, dancing and singing, sleeping by day and wandering about at night, bad companions, and avarice—these six things bring a man to ruin.

Woe to the dicers, to them that drink strong drink, that go in unto their neighbour's wife: whoso follows wickedness and honours not the wise, he shall fade like the waning moon.

He that drinks strong drink is needy and destitute, ever thristing with unquenchable thirst; he plunges into debt as one plunges into water, and will quickly bring his family to nothing.

He who sleeps by day and rises at night, who is ever full of wine and whoredoms, is unfit to maintain a family.

Poverty overtakes him who says, 'Tis too cold, 'tis too hot, 'tis too late, and neglects his daily work; but he who, performing his manly duties, recks not a straw for heat or cold, his happiness shall not decay.

There are four, young man, who, seeming to be friends, are enemies in disguise—the rapacious friend, the man of much profession, the flatterer, and the dissolute companion.

In four ways the rapacious man may be known to be a false friend: He enriches himself at your expense, he expects much in return for little; he does what is right only under the impulse of fear: and he serves you form self-interested motives.

In four ways the man of much profession may be known to be a false friend: He boasts of what he meant to have done for you; he boasts of what he means to do for you; he is profuse in unprofitable compliments, but in the hour of need he protests his inability to serve you.

In four ways the flatterer may be known to be a false friend: He assents when you do wrong; he assents when you do right; he praises you to your face; and speaks ill of you behind your back.

In four ways the dissolute companion may be known to be a false friend: He is your friend if you follow after strong drink, if you wander about the streets at night; he is your companion in threatre-going, he is your companion in dicing.

The rapacious friend, the insincere friend, the friend who speaks only to please, and he who is a companion in vicious pleasures—recognizing these four to be false friends, the wise man flies far from them as he would from a road beset with danger.

These four, young man, are true friends—the watchful friend, the friend who is the same in prosperity and adversity, the friend who gives good advice, and the sympathizing friend.

In four ways the watchful friend may be known to be a true friend: He protects you when you are off your guard; he watches over your property when you are careless; he offers you an asylum in time of danger; and when work has to be done, he gives you the means of doubling your wealth.

In four ways the friend who is the same in prosperity and adversity may be known to be a true friend: He confides to you his own secrets; he faithfully keeps yours; he forsakes you not in trouble; and he will lay down his life for your sake.

In four ways the good counsellor may be known to be a true friend: He restrains you from vice; he exhorts you to virtue; he imparts instruction, and points the way to heaven.

In four ways the sympathizing friend may be known to be a true friend: He grieves over your misfortunes; he rejoices in your happiness; he restrains those who speak ill of you; he applauds those who speak well of you.

The watchful friend, the steadfast friend, the good counsellor, and the sympathizing friend—recognizing these four to be true friends, the wise man cleaves to them as the mother cleaves to her infant son.

The wise man, endowed with righteousness, shines like a flaming fire. He who gathers wealth as the bee gathers honey, his wealth shall accumulate as the ant's nest is built up; and with wealth thus acquired, he will bring no dishonour upon his family. Let him apportion his property into four, and so let him cement friendships. With one portion let him maintain himself; with two let him carry on his business; the fourth let him treasure up; it will serve him in time of trouble.

But in what way does the disciple of holy sages guard the six quarters? Know, young man, that these are the six quarters. Parents are the east quarter, teachers are the south quarter, wife and children are the west quarter, friends and companions are the north quarter, spiritual pastors are the zenith, and servants and dependents are the nadir.

In five ways, young man, a son should minister to his parents, who are the east quarter. He should say, I will support them who have supported me, I will perform their duties, I will guard their possessions, I will make myself worthy to be their heir, and when they are gone I will pay honour to their memory. And in five ways the parents show their affection for their son. They keep him from vice, they train him in virtue, they provide him with a good educaton, they unite him to a suitable wife, and in due time make over to him the family heritage. And thus is the east quarter guarded and free from danger.

In five ways the pupil should honour his teachers, who are the south quarter. By rising in their presence, by ministering to them, by obeying them, by supplying their wants, and by attentively receiving their instruction. And in five ways the teachers show their affection for their pupil. They train him up in all that is good, they teach him to hold fast knowledge, they instruct him in science and lore, they speak well of him to his friends and companions, and protect him from danger in every quarter.

In five ways should the wife, who is the west quarter, be cherished by her husband. By treating her with respect, by treating her with kindness, by being faithful to her, by causing her to be honoured by others, and by furnishing her with suitable apparel. And in five ways the wife shows her affection for her husband.She orders her household aright, she is hospitable to kinsmen and friends, she is a chaste wife, a thrifty housekeeper, and skilful and diligent in all her duties.

In five ways should the honourable man minister to his friends and companions, who are the north quarter. By liberality, courtesy, and benevolence, by doing to them as he would be done by, and by sharing with them his prosperity. And in five ways do they in their turn show their attachment for their friend. They watch over him when he is off his guard, they watch over his property when he is careless, they offer him a refuge in danger, they forsake him not in misfortune, and show kindness to his family.

In five ways the master should provide for the welfare of his servants and dependents, who are the nadir. By apportioning work to them according to their powers, by supplying them with food and wages, by tending them in sickness, by sharing with them unusual delicacies, and by granting them occasional relaxation. And in five ways do they in return testify their affection for their master. They rise before him, and retire to rest after him, they are content with what is given them, they do their work thoroughly, and they speak well of their master.

In five ways should the honourable man minister to his spiritual masters, who are the zenith. By friendly acts, by friendly words, by friendly thoughts, by giving them a ready welcome, and by supplying their temporal wants. And in six ways do they show their affection in return. They restrain him from vice, they exhort him to virtue, they are kindly affectioned towards him, they instruct him in religious truth, clear up his doubts, and point the way to heaven.

Parents are the east quarter, teachers are the south, wife and children are the west, friends and companions the north, servants and dependents are the nadir, the zenith are spiritual pastors: let a man worship these quarters, and he will bring no dishonour upon his family.

The wise man who lives a virtuous life, gentle and prudent, lowly and teachable—such a one shall be exalted. If he be resolute and diligent, unshaken in misfortune, persevering and wise, such a one shall be exalted. Benevolent, friendly, grateful, liberal, a guide, instructor, and trainer of men—such a one shall attain honour.

Liberality, courtesy, benevolence, unselfishness, under all circumstances and towards all men—these qualities are to the world what the linchpin is to the rolling chariot. And when these qualities are wanting, neither father nor mother will receive honour and support from a son. And because wise men foster these qualities, therefore do they prosper and receive praise.

When Buddha had thus spoken the young householder Sigala addressed him as follows:—It is wonderful, Master! it is wonderful, Master! 'Tis as if one should set up again that which is overthrown, or should reveal that which is hidden, or should direct the wanderer into the right path, or hold out a lamp in the darkness—so that they that have eyes to see shall see. Yea, even thus has the Blessed Lord made known the Truth to me in many a figure. And I, even I, do put my trust in Thee, and in thy Law and in thy Church—receive me, Lord, as thy disciple and true believer from this time forth as long as life endures.

The End